Matthew Harrison

Judicial Misconceptions Shattered

The Truth About the Justice System and Help to Avoid Wrongful Convictions

Copyrights

MATTHEW HARRISON
INSPIRATIONAL BOOKS

Contents

Introduction

H ave you ever been arrested or been through the justice system before? If not, you might be like I was before I had my own first-hand experience with the law. Before my arrest, I just assumed that everything the police did was right and that everyone they arrested had to be guilty of a crime. I never once contemplated the possibility that those who are sworn to uphold and protect might actually not always do that. Nor did I ever consider that the lawyers, judges, and detectives who work on these criminal cases may not always be in search of the truth as much as they are in a high conviction rate and making money. It had never crossed my mind that the system we have currently might get it wrong more than people realize. As you read my book, you will begin to see that though our system is better than most in the world, those who are tasked with executing the law often put their own self-interests ahead of truth and justice. After my own experiences, I felt compelled to dispel some of these common misconceptions about the legal system and help others avoid some of the mistakes I made along the way.

Whether you are going through the criminal justice system for the first time or have been through the process before, it is a difficult and stressful journey. My goal in writing this book was to help those who go through the system to have a basic understanding of how it works, some of the fundamental rights of the accused, and how to prepare yourself for each step along the way. Your best defense is to know what your rights are, hire a competent attorney, and be involved in the process the entire way. Every state has different laws and statutes, so doing your homework to know what those rights are can help you ensure they are protected. This will be one of the hardest things you might ever go through, but if you are prepared, you will avoid careless mistakes and know what to do to get the best possible outcome for your case.

For those who get convicted, my book also serves as an introduction to the realities of prison life and how to navigate the various elements you will encounter. Prison is a major adjustment from your previous life, so it will take time to adjust to not being in control of when you eat, what you eat, and almost every other aspect of freedom you once enjoyed. Many experience depression and anxiety and struggle to adapt to their new reality. I think it is normal for most to experience some or all of these feelings. But you can overcome these feelings by finding worthwhile projects to do while in prison. For me, I wrote books, fought my conviction, and spent time reading books that helped enhance my understanding of God, life, and behaviors I had struggled with in the past. For others, it might be getting an education or learning a trade. Whatever it is, make it a point to have a purpose while incarcerated and set goals to achieve. Those who do find that their time has left them better able to cope with the challenges that prison presents each day are better prepared to transition back into their lives once released.

Most importantly, make your time in prison mean something. Become the person you need to be to stay out of the legal system. Your children, family, and friends need you in their lives and to help raise and support them. Do not give up when times get hard; instead, let those times motivate you and strengthen your determination to leave prison and never come back.

Chapter 1

Myths of the Judicial System

INTRODUCTION

L aw enforcement officers, judges, and those in the criminal justice system have a very difficult job. I have a lot of respect for those who protect and serve in honorable and dignified ways. But the truth is that not all in law enforcement and the judicial system are respectable, or honest, and the legal system doesn't always get it right. For those reasons, I felt it was important to help people understand what to expect if they are ever approached by law enforcement or are facing the legal system for the first time. It is important that people understand how the process works, what to expect, and also to dispel some of the myths associated with the legal system. Also crucial to know is how to protect yourself and your rights, especially if you are innocent of any crime. This is not going to be based on many legal grounds or arguments but rather on my experience and that of others who have dealt with law enforcement and have been in the legal system. Practical experience is sometimes the best teacher.

Myth #1: If the police arrest someone, that person must be guilty of a crime.

First, I want to dispel some of the myths surrounding the criminal justice system. The first is that if the police arrest someone, they must be guilty of a crime. If you were anything like me before I was arrested for a crime I did not commit, you probably believed that when the police came to arrest a person, they had to be guilty. You might also have felt the same way when seeing a mugshot on TV with the police's version of the story being told. Then, if the person went to trial and got convicted, you might have been convinced there was no doubt that that person was guilty, right? That's how I thought before I went through the criminal justice system and witnessed firsthand how incorrect my assumptions were.

Without knowing how the system works, it is easy to assume the worst about those who are portrayed in such a negative light. Sadly, in the world today, perception is a reality for many. For 39 years, this is what I thought when someone was arrested or on the news accused of a crime. Only after I was falsely accused and arrested did I realize that the system that I once thought always got it right did, in fact, get it wrong more than I ever realized. In actuality only one side of the story is told on the news and by the police, and one side of a story is never the whole story. That story may or may not be true or based on the facts. Instead, it is often just a means used by law enforcement to destroy the reputation and perception of the accused and to win the court of public opinion. Because the general public believes much of what they see on the news, if someone appears on TV with a mugshot, most believe that person is already guilty. Within hours of my arrest, my mugshot was broadcast all over the news with a story that was full of lies, distorted facts, and falsehoods—and that painted me to be a monster. There was no attempt at sticking to the facts, just a concerted effort to turn people against me with outrageous lies. Without both sides of a story, it is impossible to know whether someone is guilty or innocent. Each deserves to have his or her story told. The presumption of innocence is a right that each of us should hold dear. But sadly, in our current criminal justice system, this right is not being afforded to many who are already convicted in the court of public opinion before they ever enter a courtroom.

Myth #2: Once arrested, you can defend yourself and have your day in court.

Myth #1 leads to another myth that once you are arrested, you will have the opportunity to defend yourself and have your day in court. Here is the reality: Once you are arrested, your entire life gets turned upside down, especially if you are charged with a serious offense. The first thing that happens is that you lose your job and your credibility, especially if your arrest ends up on the news and all over social media, as mine did. The day after I was arrested, my employer was contacted and the nature of my charge was disclosed. I was immediately terminated, and all of my work assets were seized. After only one day, my livelihood was gone, and regardless of the outcome of my case, I was not going to be able to get my job back. This loss directly impacted my ability to pay for a competent attorney and was the first step to limiting my options when it came to defending myself. Then, while you sit awaiting arraignment and an opportunity to get a bond, the rest of your life gets systematically torn apart by people who assume the police are telling the truth and that you must be guilty because you have been accused. But not all who are arrested are guilty, and the system often does not treat you as innocent until proven guilty. Instead, it is the complete opposite.

That was my experience when I was arrested. The police came to my door at 6 am and arrested me in front of my young children, traumatizing them. One of my daughters continues to suffer from PTSD as a result of the trauma that day. I felt I did also for many months afterward, often hearing her screams over and over in my mind and replaying the scene in my head. It was a very scary and heart-wrenching experience that is still difficult to think about. My attorney, who had spoken to the police prior to my arrest, had indicated that if I were to be arrested, the police would arrange a time for me to turn myself in. But instead, they came to my house unannounced, traumatized my family, treated me as if I were guilty, and did not afford me the courtesy that they had previously agreed to. Then, they made sure to keep the interior light in the car on as they left my neighborhood so that all who happened to be watching could see who they arrested. As soon as they left the neighborhood, they turned the light off. I felt this was done simply to humiliate me and my family.

Myth #3: If you have never been convicted of a crime, you will be able to bond out of jail.

Another falsehood that many incorrectly assume is that if you have never been convicted of a crime, you will be able to bond out of jail and have nothing to worry about. Many do get bonds and are released to fight their cases as free men and women. However, the reality is that no one can predict who will get a bond because some who get a bond do so despite lengthy prison records and heinous crimes committed. When I went for my bond hearing, my family was in the courtroom waiting for my hearing and watched as a man who was accused of shooting a store clerk in the face and then stealing his car was released on bond, in spite of the lengthy prison record he had and the heinous crimes he had been accused of. Seeing this, my family felt if he could get a bond, surely I should be able to also. I had been told that if I had never been arrested, had a house, family, and stable job, I should get a bond. I was not a danger to the community, and there was no evidence I had committed a crime. Everything was circumstantial. But in the end, none of those things mattered to the judge who denied my bond request. She did end up granting bonds to the others who were waiting with me to see that same judge. They collectively had been accused of rape, murder, robbery, aggravated assault, and other such offenses. My offense was no worse than any of the others who received a bond that day, and all had prior convictions, and yet they all received a bond, and I did not. One might wonder how people charged with those types of crimes could get a bond, and I could not. This is the problem with the system as it stands today. There is no uniformity in how bonds are issued, and they don't apply the guidelines equally to all. Race, gender, and other biases taint how people are treated. People with long criminal records are being set free, while first-time offenders are being held without bond. It made no sense to me then, and to this day, I still do not understand

Myth #4: Lawyers are looking out for your best interests.

Another myth that people should understand is that you should never assume that attorneys are looking out for your best interests. When you experience the legal system and get arrested for the first time, it can be scary and overwhelming. You worry about your family, your job, and what people will think once they hear about your arrest. You feel helpless and desperate to get out and figure out what to do. During this desperate time, (lawyers) attorneys are quick to take advantage of your crisis and offer their services. They are reassuring and confident and tell you what you want to hear, so you will hire them—and pay large sums of money upfront to get you out of jail. It all sounds great until they receive payment from you, and then everything changes. Excuses are made when they struggle to secure your release, which they promised would be a formality. They complain that the judge was in a bad mood, the district attorney has a vendetta against them for some unknown reason, or you just got locked up at a bad time, or they were cracking down on people committing crimes like the one you were accused of and were making an example out of you. Every one of these excuses was given to me and others to whom I have spoken after they paid attorneys who promised to get them out of jail or have their cases dismissed if they were hired.

Not all attorneys behave in such unethical and despicable ways, but you must be careful in whom you select to represent you and make sure you do your homework on them, not just take them at their word. I will discuss this further when I talk about how to select a good attorney. I had three atttorneys represent me during my time in jail and prison. The first two were corrupt and lied about their abilities and capabilities. After they were paid, they did little-to-no work to represent me, prepare for trial, or protect my rights and best interests. In fact, the attorncys I paid to represent me ended up helping the prosecution ensure I was convicted by agreeing to withhold evidence that would have exonerated me in the form of text messages that directly refuted the victim's claims and testimony. Those texts also contained a confession that the story was made up and that the victim was lying about the entire incident. The jury never saw or was made aware of those texts, nor were they shown video evidence that also proved their story was made up.

My last attorney was from the public defender's office and did a great job bringing to light all the evidence that was not presented at trial or at the motions hearing for a new trial. She was able to read the text messages, provide expert testimony refuting all the medical claims made, and reveal that the prosecution had also withheld medical records that would have refuted some of the victim's claims. In the end, the judge, without explanation, still denied my new trial request.

This is quite indicative of how many innocent people are treated in our legal system today. Unfortunately, the truth, justice, and protection of those who are innocent from being convicted by the false and malicious testimony of others that is unsupported by facts are no longer the priorities of those who are elected to uphold the laws and seek justice. Far too many people now are going to prison simply because the prosecutors feel confident they can get a conviction by any means necessary, and the judges allow them too much freedom to abuse their power. As a result, far too many attorneys nowadays are not interested in pursuing justice but instead want to have high conviction rates and win at all costs, even if that means convicting innocent people.

Myth #5: You are innocent until proven guilty.

The presumption of innocence is a fundamental right for all who are accused of a crime. Everyone deserves their day in court to be able to present their side of the story and have all the facts and relevant information heard by a jury of their peers. Until that time, judgment should be reserved and each person accused should be treated fairly under the law.

But this is not how it works anymore in our justice system. With the advent of news platforms and social media that broadcast sensational one-sided stories that only tell what they think has happened without waiting for all the facts to be revealed, people too often are perceived as guilty before ever stepping foot in the courtroom. Media coverage always favors law enforcement's version of the case. Because the defense often cannot comment due to the pending litigation, the stories portray those accused as guilty. I had this experience when I was arrested. Several hours after my arrest, my daughter saw the story on the news, with outrageous claims of what I had allegedly done, having no facts or verifiable information to go on. It was the story being told by the district attorney's office, and it was full of lies and false claims, along with misconstrued information that made me out to be a monster. There was no attempt at finding the truth; their only desire was to vilify me and destroy my reputation by turning the public against me.

They did this again by petitioning to have cameras present in the court-room for every preceding I had up until the trial, and during the trial also. The decision to have media present in the courtroom is up to the presiding judge's discretion. The judge has the responsibility to determine whether the defendant would be harmed by the coverage and the jury tainted before the trial ever begins. They weigh these concerns against the public's right to information. High-profile cases, or the ones that make news headlines, are the cases that are affected most due to the jurors who are tainted by biased news coverage of the case and information that they see on social media, internet sources, and from people they talk to.

When it came time to pick a jury, many of the potential jurors we spoke to had heard of the case because of the media coverage and had already made up their minds about my guilt. Some even became enraged and said they could not even look at me because of what they had already determined I had done. With all the different ways to get news and information at the touch of a button, it is increasingly difficult to find people who have not been influenced by the news they see and hear every day. One of the jurors who had been selected in my case, as her name was called to come and sit in the jury box, turned to the woman next to her and mouthed the words, "I am going to get him." She ended up being the jury foreperson, and she did indeed "get me" as she stated she would. To this day, I still do not know what made my case so high profile. I suspect that the district attorney's office made a call to the news networks after I was arrested to ensure it was broadcast everywhere to help them achieve their purposes. Whether that is fair or right to do is a fair debate. But one of the consequences for people accused of a crime is that the presumption of innocence that we are afforded by law, is no longer being afforded to people in the justice system. Today, social media and the news media ensure that those who are arrested are guilty right from the start, and now the accused must prove their innocence or be sent to prison regardless of truth or innocence.

Myth #6: Getting a paid attorney will guarantee you get the best representation.

There is a false notion out there that if you spend enough money on an attorney, you will be able to beat your case. I admit that I felt the same way after watching a few high-profile cases in which very wealthy and well-known sports figures and movie stars won cases that all who were aware of the evidence and facts of the case felt they were guilty. High-powered attorneys who knew how to manipulate the jury and twist even the strongest evidence into appearing weak seemed to win no matter if their client really was guilty. These cases gave people like me the idea that if you get a high-priced lawyer, you are going to be fine.

What I have learned now that I have been through many attorneys and spoken to hundreds of others who have also had similar experiences to mine is that most attorneys, regardless of price, are not worth the money they are paid, especially in criminal law. Most want all or some of the money upfront for promises they have made and then deliver very little. Many set the price based on the severity of the crime and then literally do the minimum required by the judge for your case. Others simply want you to plead guilty to avoid a trial and having to do any actual work. Two of the three lawyers I had fell into these categories. Many grand promises were made, like getting me out on bond, beating my case, how many cases like mine they have fought and won, etc. But after the money was received, I barely heard from my attorneys, and then only to pay them more money. In the end, the best attorney I had was a public defender who told me everyone deserves a good defense, and that was what she was going to give me. And she did indeed. Though we did not get the desired outcome in my case, she did everything in her power to bring the truth to light and to hold my previous attorneys accountable for their mishandling of my case. The bottom line is this: you always want to look into attorneys' claims before you hire them. Paying a lot of money does not ensure you are getting a competent attorney who will work your case, but doing your homework will give you the chance to find a good one. Actions always speak louder than words, so look for an attorney who can back up their claims their their actions.

Myth #7: If you are innocent, you have nothing to worry about.

People mistakenly assume that just because they are innocent, they have nothing to worry about and that, eventually, they will be set free. In many cases, that may be true, but more often than some might realize, it is not. In the criminal justice system today, the truth and being innocent does not always guarantee you will not be convicted. When I was arrested, I was in shock, confused, and frightened that it ever got to that point to begin with. But even then, I felt that the truth would come out, and eventually, I would be free again. I knew I had not committed a crime, but I did not realize that the people who were prosecuting my case did not care about my guilt or innocence; they only seemed to be concerned with winning at all costs, regardless of whether I actually did anything wrong.

My first attorney told me that even if I didn't commit the crime, the prosecution made a comment to him that my being with someone I should not have been with while being married justified them in pursuing my case based on my infidelity. In essence, they rationalized that it was just fine to pursue me for a crime I did not commit because I was unfaithful in my marital relationship. Such justifications and excuses are used to justify pursuing cases at all costs, even those that they know are innocent of any crime. Pursuing someone for a crime they did not commit in order to punish them for things that some deem unacceptable but not criminal is an example of how the law is being abused by those in authority. I was also made aware after my trial was over that the prosecutor's office and a civil attorney whom they referred their client to had made a deal to file a civil lawsuit after the trial for 25 million dollars. This same civil attorney had been accused of giving money under the table to prosecutors who refer clients to him and help him win his cases. After doing some research, my attorney felt very confident this was also happening in my case, but we could find no other evidence to support our theory other than the fact that the civil lawyer was provided key evidence that by law was not to be released to him until after the trial was over. We had proof he was given access to the evidence months before the trial even began, but they were careful to cover their other tracks, and we could find no other evidence. Then when my attorney called them to the stand, each one of them lied and denied they had made any such arrangements.

In the end, unethical attorneys and judges do not always uphold the law in truth and fairness to those accused of crimes. They let public perceptions, race, gender, and other social issues cloud their own judgment. My case took place during a time of social movements that were advocating for all who were accused of sexual crimes to face more severe punishments. Those accused of sexual crimes during this time only needed to be accused of the crime to lose their jobs, have their names slandered over the internet, their lives threatened, and their reputations destroyed. This was all done simply by a person making an accusation and without providing any evidence to support their claims. Today, that is all that is needed to get a person convicted, one person's word against another's. Understandably, laws were being tightened against those who actually had committed crimes against women, and rightfully so. But for those who were innocent, social movements such as this one made it even more difficult to get a fair and equitable hand from the justice system. What happens in society directly affects what the law is doing and how it is enforced. The fact is, once you are accused of a crime, it is not popular in our society to let a person go free, especially after the public is led to believe that the person is guilty.

For all of these and other reasons, it is important that those who are innocent do not just assume things will somehow work out in the end. You must take all precautions you can to ensure you protect your rights, and do not assume the system will eventually get it right. You must be the one to advocate for all rights and your due process to be respected. You need to be actively engaged in ensuring the truth and all the facts come to light so that justice can be served.

Myth #8: You will be safe in the criminal system.

The assumption that you will be safe and protected while your legal process plays out is a false one. In jails and prisons across the country, people are being fatally injured and hurt at levels that are hard to fathom. Regrettably, many are being told that it is safe by those who are charged with protecting the inmates, but they know better and simply tell the public what they want to hear—even though they know the reality is something totally different. To avoid the public getting alarmed or panicked, correctional departments have gone to great lengths to cover up those who are fatally harmed by other inmates, suicides, or other fatalities resulting from drug overdoses and other self-inflicted causes. Some prison systems go so far as to not report the death of a loved one for months so that the cause of death cannot be determined. Those who have been to prison and those who have worked in a jail or prison facility can attest to the dangerous and volatile circumstances that inmates face in custody.

When I was arrested, I went to a jail that had the reputation of being the worst in the state. Gangs, violence, and filthy prison conditions were just a few of the perks of being in this notorious facility. When I first arrived and was booked into the jail, I was placed in a holding cell that had feces and urine all over the walls and floor and such an awful smell I could not eat when I was given food to eat. When I was taken to the floor I was to be housed on, we were locked down 22 to 23 hours a day due to violence and staff shortages. The reality is you are mostly on your own when you get to jail or go to prison. Most staff members are female and will not help you if you get into a fight or a riot breaks out. In my time in county jail, a guard brought a prisoner a gun so he could shoot another prisoner. He did and killed him. I witnessed numerous fights that went on for long periods of time before any officers came in to break it up. In prison, I have seen firsthand people being stabbed, attacked, beaten, and robbed without the staff doing anything to stop it.

Lately, inmates have been taking other inmates hostage, tying them up in their cells, and then beating them. Then they call the family of the inmate and attempt to extort them by telling them things like, "We will pull a tooth an hour if you don't pay us." Or "We will kill your son if you do not pay within the hour." Some pay, some do not; but those who don't end up dead or in the hospital, and those (that) who do continue to be extorted because (they) inmates know they will pay. This happens because the prisons and jails are severely understaffed, and the guards are afraid to get involved or are being paid off by the very inmates who are committing the atrocities against other inmates. I have even been told that many of the guards are affiliated with some of the gang elements that are in the prisons and jails and, therefore, help them have opportunities to do these things.

Myth #9 The Justice System is fair and equitable to all.

The last myth I want to make people aware of is that the justice system is not fair and equitable to all. For many reasons, the system we have now is unfair and broken. Depending on where you live in the country, you might face discrimination based on your race, gender, or ethnicity. You also may be discriminated against because of social status, where you live, or the education you have attained. I feel as though I faced many of these factors in my time in jail and prison.

When I was preparing to go in front of the judge for my case, I was told the judge did not like white, middle-class, educated men. My attorney, who knew the judge well, said that the judge did not like men like me because we were educated and should know better than to break the law. Therefore, before I was ever in front of the judge and before any evidence was presented, my judge was biased against me because of those factors mentioned. Her disdain for me was evident throughout the process as she denied my bail, denied every motion filed by my attorneys, and then denied my new trial motion. The judge was given compelling evidence, including a confession by the accuser that the story she told in court was a lie and many other "confessions" that were revealed from texts omitted during the trial. Her bias against me kept her from doing what was just and right in my case, and I felt that it had everything to do with my race, education, and gender. Conversely, those of different races and with lengthy prison records were given bonds and new trials by the same judge who presided over my case. It is clear that though they are not supposed to be biased toward people and judge each case based on its merits, many are influenced by their own biases and do not consistently fairly adjudicate each case.

FUTURE OF THE JUDICIAL SYSTEM

The myths in this chapter are just some common misconceptions of people who have never experienced the justice system before. What they see in movies, on the news, and what they read in the newspapers does not accurately portray what the system is really like and the challenges people face once caught up in the judicial web. Some are fortunate to have competent and ethical attorneys and judges who are fair and just in their dealings as they preside. But there is an increasing number of those who do not. I have spoken to others who have had similar experiences to mine and witnessed many other instances where injustices have occurred for the same reasons I mentioned.

The laws as they were originally have been changed and altered so that it gives an unfair advantage to one side to ensure that those who are accused of certain crimes have a harder time defending themselves from false accusations. The crime I was accused of fell into that category, and the same things that the prosecution used against me were off limits to use against the accuser, who had a history of bad behaviors that would have given the jury pause as to the veracity of her story. But those things that were used to vilify me were off limits to use against the accuser, making it difficult to show this pattern of behavior by the accuser that was highly questionable and proved in many instances the inconsistencies in the story that was presented. But because the laws have been altered in such a way as to make it impossible to show what the other person is capable of, it creates many opportunities for injustices to take place. This happens in all areas of the criminal justice system. The alteration of laws and the changes in societal norms and standards have made the way the law is applied different today than it was even 20 years ago. Knowing this is important because you do not want to put yourself in situations where you have to go through the criminal justice system today because there is no guarantee anymore that if you are innocent of a crime, you will not find yourself convicted and sent to prison.

Chapter 2

Talking With the Police

I t seems counterintuitive not to help or assist the police when investigating a crime. Most want to do their part as good citizens to help apprehend those breaking the law. However, when you are being investigated, the last thing you want to do is talk to the police, especially without an attorney. There are many reasons why this is not beneficial, but the most important thing to remember is that speaking to the police can never help you; it only hurts you.

Why do the police want to talk to me?

The police are contacting you because they are investigating a potential crime that has been committed. Your name has somehow been given to the police as a potential witness or suspect in that crime. The police want to speak to you to find out where you were at the time of the incident and what your connection may be to the case. They are also looking for more evidence that can be used against you to make an arrest.

Can I refuse to talk to the police?

You have the right to refuse to speak to the police. You also have the right not to incriminate yourself. The right to remain silent is a fundamental right all people have to avoid making any statements that can be used against them. Too often, people mistakenly say things that can be twisted, taken out of context, and used against them. Because the police are highly trained in the area of interrogation and in manipulating people, it is always best not to talk at all or at least wait until an attorney is present to advise you. Don't try to handle a police interrogation on your own, or you might unintentionally do more damage than good.

If I am innocent, I should talk to the police, right?

I once thought that if you had nothing to hide, you should not fear speaking to the authorities. After all, they are just trying to get to the truth and find the person responsible, right? Wrong. Perhaps back 50 years ago, that may have been true, but that is not true today. Many, if not most, of law enforcement nowadays use tactics that are designed to get people to admit to all kinds of things—even things they haven't done in an effort to get convictions. The search for truth and justice has given way to conviction rates and the perception that law enforcement is doing its job, even at the expense of the innocent people they are sending to prison as a result of not doing proper investigations.

I have heard of and seen many examples of this in my time in prison. An example of this happened to a man charged with the sexual assault of a woman he met briefly at work. One evening, they were together, and then he took her home. The next day he was contacted by law enforcement because the woman claimed he raped her the night before. Anxious to clear his name, he voluntarily went to speak to the police. They were able to get a DNA sample during the interview to rule him out as a suspect, according to the police. However, a short time later, he was arrested and charged with the crime. The police did not disclose the results of the DNA testing until very close to the trial. When the results came back, the man they had arrested for the crime did not match the DNA taken from the victim. Rather than continue to investigate to find the person responsible, the police instead prosecuted and convicted the innocent man they had arrested based on circumstantial evidence and witness testimony. These kinds of breakdowns in investigations are seen each day on the news as people who had been convicted of crimes years before are being exonerated by new evidence that was never presented at their trials.

How many lives have been destroyed by haphazard police investigations that were not thorough or accurate? Desperate to clear cases and to appease the public, more and more cases are being prosecuted not based on the truth, facts, or evidence but rather on the abilities of the police and prosecution to tell a believable story and have witnesses who will falsely testify to it. Once a person comes in for an interview, the police employ a variety of tactics, including deception, intimidation, sleep deprivation, hunger, fear, and threats of increased prison time to illicit confessions to the crimes they are investigating. Many men whom I have spoken with have recounted stories of talking to the police to clear their names and have instead been charged with the crime. Most have said the police used the tactics above to get them to say things that were then used to arrest them and ultimately convict them.

It also works the same for those innocent witnesses who come to speak to the police to share their stories relevant to the case. The detectives will use many different tactics to get these witnesses to testify to what they want their story to be. They use deception, scare tactics, and reassurances that if they testify, nothing bad will happen to them. In my case, the recorded interviews with potential witnesses were filled with detectives lying to potential witnesses, stating I was knowingly giving people STDs, physically assaulting people, and that they would be preventing others from similar fates. The truth was that the police already had proof that I had no STDs and that I had not physically harmed anyone. These lies instead were used to scare and convince others to falsely testify against me. Then, their testimonies were manipulated until they closely matched those of others who were to testify so they could establish a pattern of behavior. Some of the witnesses interviewed did not want to testify but were deliberately deceived into testifying by the detectives, telling them I would take a plea if enough people were willing to testify. I did not take a plea, and they all were forced to testify, willingly or not.

No matter if you are an innocent witness or potential suspect, law enforcement will use whatever means necessary to ensure the outcome it wants. Even innocent witnesses are often manipulated into saying what the prosecution wants in order to suit their purposes. I have spoken to others who went to speak to the police and had absolutely nothing to do with the crime but came away almost convinced that they did somehow after speaking to the detectives. Because they are trained in these techniques, someone who is unfamiliar with these tactics can easily fall victim to their ploys and unwittingly say things that the police then twist to fit their narrative and end up arrested for something they did not do. No matter if you are innocent or guilty, it is never in your best interest to speak to the police.

What if my attorney is present during questioning?

Any good attorney will tell you never to talk to the police. Once you hire an attorney, that person will communicate with the police. Because attorneys have a knowledge of the law and tactics used by law enforcement, they can protect you from saying or doing something that could potentially make you vulnerable to prosecution. However, there are some circumstances where it may be appropriate to speak to the police with your attorney present. In these circumstances, it is important to pause after the detectives ask a question and look to your attorney before answering. Your attorney will help you to know what you can and cannot say and safeguard against incriminating yourself. When I tell you that talking to the police is never a good idea, I am not trying to suggest that the police are out to get everyone or that there are not good and honest law enforcement everywhere, but rather this is simply to protect you and your rights because you don't always know what the intentions are of those you might speak with.

By maintaining your right to remain silent, you are safeguarding your most important right when being investigated for a crime. Also, having a competent attorney will help ensure that you will be prepared for each step along the process and protected from the various tactics that law enforcement uses—especially on people not familiar with how the system works.

The entire reason that the police are interviewing you is that they lack the evidence to arrest you. The point of the interview is to get enough evidence to make an arrest. Knowing this ahead of time, you can see why it is not in your best interest to speak to them about any investigation they may be looking into. Instead, you should remain silent. Then, if necessary, get an attorney to speak to the police for you. Statements made by your attorney cannot be used against you in court, only your statements can. As a defendant, you do not want to say anything that can and most certainly will be used against you in court. Knowing why you are being questioned and the purpose of police interrogations will protect you and help you be prepared if and when the police ever contact you. Just remember that talking to the police can only harm you, not help you. Now, you might need a few tips on finding a competent attorney, and that is what we will discuss in the next chapter.

Chapter 3

Finding A Competent Attorney

W hen looking for an attorney, you will find many options. Most will tell you they know exactly what to do and have had many cases similar to yours; and if you go ahead and pay them, they will get to work on your case immediately. In other words, they tell you what you want and need to hear in your time of crisis and fear so they can get paid. But I and many others have learned from very painful experiences that choosing an attorney is critical to achieving the best outcome for your case and is, therefore, worth taking your time to ensure you have the best attorney for the job.

Note: The first thing you need to understand is that a distinction may be made between a lawyer and an attorney. A lawyer is someone who has completed a course of legal training at a law school, which usually involves three years of full-time study beyond an undergraduate degree. Both a lawyer and attorney receive legal training and have earned a Juris Doctor (JD) degree. However, every attorney is a lawyer, but not all lawyers are attorneys. Attorneys must pass the bar exam that measures knowledge and competence to practice law. The American Bar Association does not differentiate between the two terms and uses the terms interchangeably to refer to a person who can practice law. However, some law offices may use attorneys to refer to people who have different responsibilities or specializations. For example, they may use the word *attorney* to describe a person whose typical work involves representing people in court and use the word lawyer to describe a person who does other kinds of legal work outside of the courtroom, such as offering legal advice or reviewing legal documents. A criminal attorney has certain educational requirements. You not only have to pass exams in law school, but you must also pass other exams before you can become a criminal defense lawyer. There are ethics to uphold and subject matter to master, in addition to other subjects selected by the state's bar examiners. Continuous education is required in most states.

HOW DO YOU FIND A GOOD ATTORNEY?

There are many different ways to find good attorneys. Unfortunately for me, I learned by doing it all wrong the first few times and then figured out some things along the way. One thing to remember when speaking to attorneys is that they will always tell you what you want to hear to various extents. Many will tell you how many cases they have won, how they know certain prosecutors or judges, how they will keep you from ever being arrested, or, if arrested, will get you a bond and the best outcome for your case. But they won't tell you how hard they will work on your case, how many cases they are now working on, or how much experience they have with the crimes you are being charged. These are the things you have to research and find on your own. But thanks to the internet, social media, public court records, and past clients, you have many ways to find the information you are looking for. Here are the best places to go to do your homework on attorneys you are considering to represent you.

Court Records

Many attorneys will offer recent cases they have won similar to yours to show you how competent they are in defending those they represent. If your attorney cannot offer recent cases tried with favorable outcomes, I would be hesitant to hire that person. Because laws and statutes change frequently, without having any recent cases, your attorney may not be aware of those changes and not represent you properly. This is exactly what happened with the attorney who represented me at trial. When we contacted him to represent me, he claimed to have tried and won many cases like mine in the past few years and that he was aware of the laws and statutes of the crime I was accused of. However, we came to find out later at trial that he did not know anything about the current laws and statutes and, as a result, was ineffective in defending me. At the hearing for a new trial, he admitted on the stand that he had misrepresented his knowledge and abilities to us and had only tried one case like mine in his career—30 years previously! Had we done our homework, looked into his claims, and requested court records of cases he had tried, we could have avoided the mistake we made in hiring him. Court records are available to the public, and any potential attorney you hire should be able to give you several case numbers to research on recent cases they have tried. If they don't have any recent cases that were tried successfully, I would look elsewhere for representation.

Social Media

In this age of information, social media offers a quick way to locate information on a variety of subjects, including attorneys. When people have good attorneys and their cases are dismissed, or they win their case, you may find a few positive things about it. But if the attorney did a poor job or did not do as they claimed they would or should do, you will find many who make it known on social media. When the outcomes are good, you hear little; when they are bad, you hear a lot! Don't be afraid to google your attorney and find out what people have to say about that person! Often, you will be surprised at what you can find out about people simply by looking into them online. A caution about online searching is to determine if the site is reliable and impartial. We found after my experience that a site promising impartiality would not accept our negative review and asked us to take down the review. When we would not, they took it down against our wishes. So, the lesson learned here is that you need to consider more than one way to verify attorney competence or suffer in the long run.

Law Firm Website

Most attorneys or firms have a website that offers information on what types of law they specialize in, where the attorneys went to school, how many years they have been practicing law, and recent cases they have won. They also give the names of the attorneys and contact information, if you have questions or concerns. This is another resource to use to find the information you need in order to make an informed decision. Though the website will only display the most favorable things about its attorneys, you can still get some valuable information on cases recently worked on and their outcomes.

Online Service Providers

Many attorneys also use online companies that they pay to advertise and market their services. These websites offer customers a one-stop shop for all their legal needs. However, you must be careful using these sites because they can be very misleading and deceptive. The attorney we hired to take my case used one of these service providers. After the trial, we tried to leave a comment about his poor performance on the website so others would be aware of what he did. However, the website refused to post anything that was negative toward one of its members. So, if you use a website to research or select an attorney, be aware that you may not be getting the truth about the attorney you are looking to hire. Some websites allow only positive feedback on their clients, so you may not be getting the whole story unless you look to other sources for information. It is always better to look to many different sources to determine if the information you are getting is consistent and accurate. The websites are paid to represent the interests of their clients; in this case, those clients are the attorneys who are paying the websites to advertise their services and to protect them from negative feedback.

Friends and Coworkers

Many times, when we have a legal situation that requires the help of an attorney, friends and coworkers often know of someone in the legal profession they can recommend or refer you to. Some of them have had personal dealings with the attorney, and others just know they practice in the criminal defense field. It is great to have someone who can recommend an attorney when you are in a crisis situation, but you also need to take the same precautions with an attorney who comes recommended. The attorney I hired to defend me was recommended by a trusted friend. However, he specialized in drunk driving cases and was not what I needed. In addition to that, he was deceptive and lacked the knowledge and experience necessary to adequately defend me at trial. His insistence on my taking a plea finally made sense after I saw his performance in the courtroom. Because we trusted our friend, we failed to look into his claims of having done many cases like mine before and that he was well-versed in the laws and statutes that applied to my case. It is an easy mistake to make but a costly one for me and for my family. It is your responsibility to ensure you always look into each person you are considering to represent you because assuming someone is telling you the truth could cost you years in prison.

Can I research while I am in jail?

For many, getting arrested comes as a shock and leaves no time to find a good attorney. Many must do as I did and rely on family and friends to help you select someone to represent you. Do not panic or make decisions based on fear or desperation. You have some time, so don't rush to judgment on selecting someone to represent you. Talk with your friends and family, discuss what your options are, and ask to meet with the potential attorney before making the choice to hire. Ask all your questions and then have your family verify the details that you discuss. Remember, it is your choice on who you want to represent you, so choose someone you feel comfortable with and whom you can afford.

What if I cannot afford an attorney?

One thing I learned quickly in looking for an attorney is that they are very expensive. Depending on the severity of the crime, attorneys will charge you accordingly. The more severe the crime, the more work they potentially will have to do, making it more expensive and difficult for some to pay their legal expenses. If you find you are unable to pay, the judge can appoint a public defender to represent you instead. Court-appointed attorneys work for the state, often in the same offices as the prosecutors who are going against you. They are paid the same amount no matter what happens in your case, so it is in their best interests to have you take a plea because it is less work for them, and they get paid the same whether you take a plea or go to trial. Being aware of these things will help you avoid taking a plea simply to make your attorney's job easier. If you are innocent of the crime, it is almost always in your best interests to not take a plea because then you forfeit your rights to an appeal. Court-appointed attorneys often try to convince their clients it is better to take a plea than go to trial and risk more prison time, but many often regret making a deal once they get to prison and learn more about the process and options available to them. It is always better to protect your rights rather than surrender them to those who have no incentive to fight for you.

Public defenders also have a bad reputation for being bad attorneys. Many are overwhelmed with cases and try their best to get people to simply take a plea to lessen their loads and to keep their caseloads manageable. Some are good and work hard to defend those whom they are assigned to help to the best of their ability. My appellate attorney was from the public defender's office. After spending all the money we had on paid attorneys, we had no choice but to ask the judge to appoint an attorney to help with my appeal. Though I was leery of having a court-appointed attorney for such an important part of my appeal process, she worked harder than either of my first two paid attorneys and brought much of the truth of my case to light. She told me everyone deserves to have good representation, and no matter their guilt or innocence, she was going to provide that. I greatly appreciated her work and efforts on my behalf.

Others who have had public defenders have not been so lucky. Many seem to lack concern about their clients or their best interests. I have witnessed personally how they attempt to get people to take pleas, regardless of guilt or innocence. I have also seen them take advantage of people whose English is not their native language to have them plead guilty to crimes that they did not commit. I came to know a man in prison who had a public defender who made no effort to help him; he just had him sign a plea and go to prison because someone had sent an email saying he had committed a crime. That was all the evidence they had on him. Sadly his story is like hundreds of others I have heard about or seen in my time in prison. If you have no choice but to have the court appoint an attorney, you can still request different representation if that person is not working on your behalf. Make sure you document your requests and anything you feel your attorney is not doing and present this to the judge to help ensure you are getting competent help. Above all, do all you can to learn what your rights are and what you are entitled to so you can ensure your rights are protected and your case is fairly adjudicated.

Can I fire my attorney if that person does not work out?

Yes! You can absolutely fire an attorney who is not looking out for you or your best interests. Attorneys should be working for you; and if that is not happening, you need to look elsewhere for representation. I had to fire my first attorney because he misrepresented himself and the costs of his services. He waited until just before a court hearing to inform me that if I wanted him to represent me in the hearing that was minutes away, I needed to pay him additional money. However, when I first hired him, he stated that what I had paid to him would cover the costs through the bond hearing that I was preparing to have shortly. But at that moment, he claimed that I had not paid him enough to represent me at the bond hearing and that I needed to pay him an additional amount or he would have to withdraw representation. So, rather than being extorted for more money, I fired my attorney, and I told the judge I needed new representation. She gave me a week to do so. My trial attorney also extorted money from my family during the trial. As he was preparing to give my defense, he approached my family, unbeknownst to me, and asked them for more money. Afraid that not paying him would result in poor representation, they paid him what he wanted. I only found out about it after I was convicted and sent to prison. Because he had quoted a price that was to cover the entire case through the trial, I was shocked to learn he had taken additional money that was above and beyond what had been agreed to. But this is how many attorneys operate; consequently, you must be careful and ensure you are not being extorted or taken advantage of by knowing your rights and what to expect at each step of the process.

I had to fire my first attorney because he misrepresented himself and the cost of his services. He waited until just before a court hearing to inform me that if I wanted him to represent me in the hearing, which was minutes away,

I needed to pay him additional money. However, when I first hired him, he stated that what I paid him would cover the costs through the upcoming bond hearing. But at that moment, he claimed that I had not paid him enough to represent me at the bond hearing and that I needed to pay him an additional amount or he would have to withdraw representation. So, rather than being extorted for more money, I fired my lawyer and told the judge I needed new representation. She gave me a week to do so.

My trial lawyer also extorted money from my family during the trial. As he was preparing to give my defense, he approached my family, unbeknownst to me, and asked them for more money. Afraid that not paying him would result in poor representation, they paid him what he wanted. I only found out about it after I was convicted and sent to prison. Because he had quoted a price to cover the entire case through the trial, I was shocked to learn he had taken additional money above and beyond what had been agreed to. But this is how many attorneys operate, so you must be careful and ensure you are not being extorted or taken advantage of by knowing your rights and what to expect at each step of the process.

Because attorneys can be unscrupulous and do immoral things in their pursuit of clients and money, you must be aware of what your rights are and not be afraid to speak up if you feel you are being taken advantage of. This is why attorneys are often held in such low regard because of how frequently they take advantage of people who lack knowledge, both of the system and of the law. But do not allow a crooked and unscrupulous attorney to represent you because your life depends on you finding someone who is working for you, not against you.

Even when being as careful as you can and doing your research, there are no guarantees your attorney will do as promised and work your case honestly and diligently. But you can avoid major missteps by looking into their claims and their track record to ensure they have the expertise and knowledge they need to properly defend you. Ultimately, you have to decide who you feel will best represent you and your interests. Trust your initial instincts; they are right the majority of the time. Also, be aware that if your attorney does not do as you ask or is not working your case to your satisfaction, you may fire them and find someone else. Though it may cost you to do so, you are never forced to keep an attorney you don't like or who is not adequately representing you each step of the way.

Chapter 4

The Arrest Process

Inevitably, after the police investigate you for a crime, then comes the arrest. Sometimes the police will allow you to turn yourself in to avoid an embarrassing scene in front of your neighbors, family, or work associates. Other times, they show up unannounced early in the morning and make a spectacle in front of those you care about. That is what they did to me in the early morning hours as I was preparing to go to work. My attorney had previously arranged for me to turn myself in should that become necessary, but the police did not honor that arrangement and instead came to my home and traumatized my wife and children. Then, as an added measure of humiliation, they made sure to leave the light on in the car as we slowly drove out of my neighborhood so that anyone watching would see who they came to arrest that day. Another example of how the system allows the police to treat people like they are guilty from the start. Instead of innocent until proven guilty, you are guilty until proven innocent in the legal system today.

THE ARREST

An important thing to remember when being arrested is not to say or do anything that could lead to more charges. The police will not hesitate to add new charges to the ones they are already arresting you for should you resist them when they come to get you. If they do not read your rights to you as required by law, make a mental note not to sign your arrest paperwork and instead let your attorney know because that is a violation of your rights. Most importantly, remember that anything you say or do can be used against you. Once arrested, have someone contact your attorney or look into getting one and wait to speak to that person. Do not speak to the police or do anything that could result in more charges that make the situation worse.

BOOKING

Once arrested, you are taken to the intake portion of the jail to be booked. Being booked into jail is a discomforting process that starts with standing up against a wall to be searched. Anything like a phone, wallet, or keys is taken and then you are led to a waiting area where you will have your mugshot taken, be fingerprinted, fill out paperwork, and then be escorted to a changing area where you strip off all your clothing and jewelry, shower, and then get dressed in a jail jumpsuit. Next, you wait to have a medical exam and tests done, and then you are escorted in handcuffs to a different floor where you are housed until your initial court date. This process can be relatively long or short, depending on the day and how many are waiting to be booked.

One thing for sure is that the process is not fun, and the feelings you have as you wait your turn to have your picture taken and be fingerprinted are some you may never forget. I remember sitting in the chair, stunned and confused at the fact that I was even arrested. I kept thinking it had to be a mistake or that I was dreaming and would wake up shortly. Then, your mind inevitably turns to your family, your job, and your children and what will happen to them. You wonder what others will think of you now that you have been arrested. Will they believe anything you say going forward? It is a terrible feeling and a day I have not forgotten. But there are some things you need to try to remember when you are going through this harrowing process to ensure you protect yourself and your due process rights.

MIRANDA RIGHTS

Once you sit down in the waiting area, you will be asked to sign the paperwork for the crimes you are being charged with. At the bottom of that sheet is an acknowledgment of being given your Miranda rights, which is required by law. Your Miranda rights are the basic rights you have and are reminded of whenever you are taken into police custody. They are the following: "You have the right to remain silent. Anything you say can and will be used against you in a court of law. You have the right to an attorney, and if you cannot afford one, one will be appointed for you." Then they ask you if you understand your rights. If you are not read and afforded these rights, you need to be sure not to sign any paperwork or do anything until you speak to your attorney.

When the police came to my home to arrest me, they failed to disclose my Miranda rights as required by law because of the screams and protests of my children. Then, when I was given the arrest paperwork and told to sign it, I did so without realizing I should not have signed that form without first consulting my attorney. If I had, he would have said not to sign the paperwork because, at the bottom, it stated that my Miranda rights had been told to me by the arresting officers, which they had not. He then could have asked the judge to have my arrest thrown out and released from custody or have my case thrown out down the road because my due process rights were violated. If I had been aware of those things when I was arrested, I would have done so. But being naive to the entire process and scared and confused already, I just did what they told me to do, like so many others before me who were also ignorant of the system and the law.

SURVIVING THE PROCESS

The booking process is scary, and when you experience it for the first time, it feels overwhelming. The holding cells where I was held during booking were filthy and disgusting, with no toilet paper to use, no cups to get water, and feces smeared on the walls. This area also had people who were often drunk, high on drugs, or angry because of their current circumstances. I had one man tell me he was going to attack me because of my skin color and because he hated people who looked like me. Others threatened to take my food, which I had no appetite for anyway. You will encounter these and other things as you go through this process; however, as long as you know what to expect, you will be able to protect yourself and your rights even in those difficult circumstances.

It is also important to keep in mind that the jail I went to had the reputation for being the worst in the state. Not all will be as difficult as the one I experienced. Some will be better, and yet others will be even worse than what I have described. I have heard stories from other jails in other states where they had no running water, slept on the floor with no mattresses, blankets, or sheets to keep warm, and were in overcrowded cells where inmates had to sleep on the floor next to each other because of a lack of space. These cells were also infested with bugs and cockroaches that ran over them while they slept and food portions that were less than meager. Because jails are cramped and it is a stressful time for many, violent behavior is to be expected. Therefore. be aware of what is going on around you and stay away from volatile situations if you can.

No matter what jail you might end up in, the process is difficult and traumatizing. I wrote this book with the intent to help others facing incarceration for the first time and to prepare them and their families for what is ahead. Knowing what you are going to go through can also be hard, but that knowledge can help you safely navigate those challenges and ensure the best outcome in your situation.

Chapter 5

County Jail

After you are booked into jail and receive the one phone call you are allotted, you are then moved to the classification dorm, where you are kept a few days until you either bond out or are moved to a cell in the general population. There are a few exceptions to this. For example, if you were to request to be kept in personal protection, commonly called "PC." This is protective housing where those who fear for their life, or cannot be kept in general population go for various reasons. This does not always guarantee someone will be safe, but it does provide fewer opportunities for those looking to harm someone who is housed there. The other exception is for medical purposes. If you are a danger to yourself or have a serious medical condition or mental health problem, you might be housed in a medical so that you can be monitored. With those few exceptions, your stay in classification will last a few days, and then you will be sent to the general population.

LIFE IN JAIL

The first few days in jail are usually the worst for everyone. Being removed from your life and family and having your freedoms and dignity stripped away leave you feeling lost and abandoned. Feelings of regret and remorse for the circumstances that brought you to that point overwhelm your mind. And if that is not enough, you must now also learn a completely different routine that is difficult and uncomfortable.

ADJUSTING TO A NEW ROUTINE

The schedule and routine you are forced into in jail are very different from what you do in your normal life. One of the first things you have to adjust to is being counted six times a day. This is done either by standing next to your door or by the officers walking past your cell and shining a light in your face.

The next adjustment is your eating schedule. In jail, breakfast is served in the early morning hours, around 2 to 4 am, depending on the facility. Most also serve lunch at the same time, which may consist of two bologna sandwiches and a few cookies. That is all you will receive until around 6 to 7 pm in the evening. Breakfast is usually either oatmeal or grits, with potatoes, bread, and occasionally a small slice of sausage. Portions sizes are minimal, so being hungry all the time is also an adjustment.

On the weekends, it gets worse with some jails only serving two meals, so commissary is a great benefit if you can afford to get it, or family and friends can help out. The other change you will notice right away is the quality of food you will get in jail. Most food is overcooked, bland, and very small in portion size. You also get overwhelmed with pasta, rice, and bread, which are the staples most jails serve daily. Because your diet will be lacking from the food you are given, you will want to order vitamins from the commissary to help offset the loss of fruits and vegetables you will lack from jail menus.

COMMISSARY

The commissary is a great benefit to those who are in jail, but it comes at a cost. Commissary items are, on average, about three times the amount you pay in the store for the same item. Commissary is only available once a week, so you must anticipate your needs and be sure to get everything you will need to last until the next store day. Jails do not supply or allow some of your basic hygiene needs. Things like toothbrushes, toothpaste, floss, or other hygiene items can be purchased only through the commissary and are expensive. Many jails do not allow you to have a razor, so you end up with a beard or have to wait until you receive a haircut to have your beard shaved. Haircuts happen about once a month, but sometimes, it can be two or more, depending on staff and clipper availability. Having a commissary was a huge benefit to me because it allowed me to get some items to help with the hunger pains. It also allowed me to get paper, stamps, and envelopes to mail letters home to avoid talking about things on the phone that I did not want to discuss with the district attorney's office listening.

PHONES MONITORED

Many in jail forget that their calls are monitored and anything they say can and will be used against them in court. I saw many instances of people doing harm to their cases by saying or admitting to things on the phone while talking to loved ones. It is easy sometimes to forget that they listen to every call, especially when you are new to the environment. But you must be careful because even speaking innocently about something can result in catastrophic consequences.

One of those innocent times, I was joking with my wife about how bad the food was and that it might kill me before I had a resolution to my case. We laughed about it and were clearly joking; however, within two hours, I had officers at my cell, was handcuffed, and taken to medical on suicide watch. I was stripped of all my clothing, put in a paper gown, and placed in a cell that felt like it was close to freezing for two days. The second day, I was so cold I felt like I would not make it through another night. Thankfully, the doctor whom I spoke to realized I was joking with my wife and not suicidal. He released me after two days. However, the trauma and discomfort of that experience reminded me never to say things on the phone that can be used against me because they are listening and will use anything they can against me.

JAIL DORMS

General populations in jail usually reside in dorms of cells where there are two ranges, upper and lower. There are typically anywhere from 2 to 4 people in a cell and 40 to 60 in a dorm. Many jails have you locked down anywhere from 18 to 23 hours a day in a cell. The jail I was in allowed us out 1 to 2 hours a day to make phone calls, watch TV, shower, walk around the common area, or exercise. The rest of your day you spend in a cell either reading, sleeping, or listening to TV reality shows or writing letters. I spent my time reading and writing letters.

MEDICAL CARE

The standard of medical care given to those in jail is much lower than the care you would receive from your own doctor. Instead of being properly diagnosed, given the proper medications, and seen and treated in a timely manner, often people are misdiagnosed, not given the correct medications, and made to wait months and years to receive treatment.

One man I met while in jail came down with an illness and sought medical care. After running numerous tests, he was treated with various medications, all of which seemed to make the problem worse, not better. When he went to the see doctor to follow up on his progress, it was discovered that he had been receiving the wrong medications. Apparently, someone on the same floor but in another dorm had the same last name, and they mixed up the medications so that these men were each getting the other man's meds. Unfortunately for each of them, they both had suffered because they did not receive the proper medications for over a month. When the man from my dorm discovered what they had been giving him, he found out it was to treat HIV, and it made him very sick. The man who needed the HIV treatment also became very ill, and both men suffered for the mistakes that were made. Unfortunately what happened to those men is not an isolated incidence; it is the norm that takes place on a regular basis.

In jail, people are also more susceptible to medical issues because of a variety of factors, including poor diet, lack of exercise, stress, and poor conditions that exist in jails. To combat this, you need to find ways to exercise, eat as well as possible, and do everything you can to avoid preventable healthcare problems. There are many in prison and jails who end up developing chronic care issues that become very burdensome and can be very difficult to deal with. A large percentage of people in jail are treated for diabetes, heart disease, high cholesterol, and other problems associated with lack of exercise and poor diets. The key to avoiding these kinds of preventable health conditions is to be careful with what you eat and find ways to exercise each day. Though it is not easy to always be motivated to exercise, the benefits of it are worth all the efforts that you make.

EXERCISE AND RECREATION

Exercise and recreation are almost non-existent in many jails. Lack of staffing and violence are the reasons cited for jails restricting inmates from recreation time. For most, it is up to the individual to find ways to get the necessary exercise to stay healthy while you are fighting your case. Though it is not easy or convenient to exercise in jail, the alternative is even worse. Jails and prisons have large portions of their inmate populations with chronic diseases. To combat this, exercising for 30 to 60 minutes per day can be the difference between developing a medical condition or having relatively good health.

I found a variety of ways to exercise in my jail cell, and also in prison. I also used ideas that others had to do the necessary exercises to maintain my overall health. Watching what others do and finding exercises that work for you will help reduce stress, anxiety, and your chances for developing a chronic medical condition. Because jail is very stressful and difficult, I found exercising was a great help in reducing stress and anxiety, and I felt better overall. There is not much you can do to help yourself in jail, but exercise is one of the most beneficial for you to feel better and avoid unnecessary medical care.

JAIL CULTURE AND LANGUAGE

Jail and prison also have their own language. The first time in jail, you will hear and see things unfamiliar to you, and they will be confusing and hard to figure out. It takes time to adjust to this new world and learn how people talk and what they mean. But asking a lot of questions and paying attention to what people are saying will help you adapt quickly to the new language and environment.

The culture is also very different from the life and society that you were removed from. Jail justice is more immediate and painful if you don't learn quickly what things you can and cannot do once inside. Some things you learn quickly are etiquette while in your cell and around your cellmate and how to use the bathroom in your cell. Though these seem like small issues, many do things to upset the people they live around. If you start off on the wrong foot, you may never be able to recover. It is important to be respectful to your cellmate; do not touch or take things that are not yours, and maintain proper hygiene. Doing these things will help you get along well with the people around you. Because you are also surrounded by people of various backgrounds and ethnicities, it is helpful to learn to be respectful of others' beliefs and cultures.

In my time in jail, I took time to find out about various cultures and religions so that I could respect and speak intelligently to people around me who had different beliefs and grew up in different cultures and backgrounds. I took time to find out about these various cultures and religions so that I could respect and speak intelligently to people around me who had different beliefs and grew up in different cultures. This afforded me the opportunity to share my values and beliefs with them, and this provided mutual respect and understanding of each other. But it also created respect for one another, and that has served me well even in my prison environment. It is important to make friends and not enemies in jail and prison. Enemies can make your life difficult no matter where you go, and friends look out for you just the same.

The culture in jail is also heavily influenced by gangs and criminal organizations that use money, violence, and intimidation to control dorms and, at times, facilities. Inmates and those who run the jails acknowledge that guards and staff bring in most of the contraband in jails and prisons. These guards are well-paid to provide anything from drugs to phones and even weapons.

GANGS

Gangs also use what they call "civilians" to initiate new members into their groups. A "civilian" is a person who is not affiliated with any gang or organization. To initiate a new member, some gangs randomly pick a civilian out and beat him to become a member of the gang. Others must survive a beating at the hands of all the others in the gang at one time. Still others must go to even greater lengths, including murder, in order to join some of these organizations. Once joined, you are then asked to protect and fight for others in the group, with the promise of the same. Many join gangs to have protection on the inside, and others because they enjoy having access to the contraband and money that they get by robbing, extorting, and selling drugs, phones, and other contraband to inmates. Gangs also do their best to befriend guards so that they can use them to facilitate their purposes. I saw many examples of this in jail. I knew of guards who opened cells so inmates could rob and assault other inmates. I also knew of times when the guards left their posts, so fights could happen, and then not return to their posts until the fighting was over. I quickly learned that there are very few in positions of power that you can trust and very few who are not willing to take bribes from other inmates.

Guards also will be paid to allow some inmates certain freedoms within the dorm, like extra phone time, food, time out of their cells, and orderly duties. The county jail I was housed in was recently under investigation for an officer bringing in steak dinners to a group of inmates. It is not a secret that the only people who come and go from the jail are those who work there. They are the ones responsible for bringing in the contraband and selling it to the highest bidders. This is all part of the culture that has been in the prison system from the beginning. But many are unaware of these facts until they themselves become a part of the system, and their eyes are opened to the reality of it all. It is important to understand that jail and prison operate in a totally different world from free society. This world does not function under the same rules as normal society. Instead, it is driven by money, desire for power, and the ability that some have to control and manipulate others to do as they want. It also thrives on misinformation about what really happens on the inside versus what is being told to the public by the police and those who run the prisons and jails around the country.

The reality is many who run these jails and prisons are guilty of taking bribes themselves and, as a result, do not try to stop the flow of contraband because it would take away from the money they are getting for bringing it in. A good example of this happened during the COVID-19 pandemic. Jails and prisons around the country were locked down with no visitation or educational classes. The Department of Corrections has repeatedly stated that contraband is largely brought into the prisons by drones and visitors. However, during the Pandemic, when all visitation was suspended and inmates were locked down all day for months, there were more drugs, phones, and other contraband being sold and used than at any time I had been inside. Because the only people going in and out of the facilities during that time were staff, it was easy to see who the people were who were bringing those items in. In addition to that, it is well known by those who are responsible for these facilities that there is a major drug problem, inmates with cell phones, and other types of contraband. If they really wanted to stop it or severely restrict it, they could do so. However, instead, they allow these things to take place because it is in their best interest to do so.

It is a sad reality, but it is also the truth. For those who are coming into the system, knowing what you are dealing with will enable you to decide how you want to proceed. If you want to indulge in these things, they are here and available. If you do not, be careful whom you talk and share information with. If someone hears you tell another their secrets, that may get you hurt or worse. In like manner, if you talk to prison or jail officials and share information about other inmates, you might end up on a hit list because, in prison or jail, they do not tolerate snitching. The only people I trust here are the ones I have spent enough time around to know who they are; even then, I don't say anything that could get me put in harm's way. The best way to stay safe in jail and prison is to take care of your own business and not get involved in others' dealings.

Chapter 6

Commissary Benefits and Cautions

WHAT IS COMMISARY?

A commissary is the jail version of a store. It provides inmates with a way to purchase food, clothing, hygiene, medications, and letter-writing/mailing materials. Most facilities have a limit to the amount of money you can spend per week, but some do not. Items purchased through the commissary are often very expensive and can cost an average of three times the amount you would pay in a store for the exact same item. But because they know inmates are desperate for the items they provide, they charge an exorbitant fee to provide them. Commissary is big business for jails and prisons nationwide.

WHAT FOODS ARE AVAILABLE?

Most of the food available in the commissary is snacks, candies, and sweets. There are a few healthier options, such as tuna fish, peanut butter, and trail mix; however, the majority of the food is similar to what you would find in a vending machine or the snack section of a grocery store. Snacks such as chips, candy bars, snack cakes, and donuts are common commissary items. Most commissaries also carry an assortment of ramen noodles in various flavors, which is a staple food item in both jail and prison. It is also used for currency to buy things, as are all the items available in the commissary. Coffee, tea, sodas, and water are also available for purchase. Another type of food available is ready-to-eat meals. Noodles, pasta, and various types of meat like beef stew, roast beef and gravy, fried chicken, and spaghetti with meatballs are a few common selections. Summer sausages, meat and cheese sticks, and various fish products, such as sardines, can also be purchased. All of these meals come in a package that is designed to be heated in water in order to eat. Most jails only have hot water in the cells if at all, so inmates are forced to plug the drain in their sink to fill it with warm water to try to heat up the food before eating. Some also make heating elements to plug into an electrical outlet and then put their food in a bucket of water to heat their meals. Others would place the food package on top of a light fixture in order to heat their food. I usually preferred the light fixture because it gave off the most heat and could get the food at least lukewarm. That is about as hot as any meal gets in jail, and you get accustomed to eating cold meals as time goes on.

WHAT NONFOOD ITEMS ARE AVAILABLE?

Hygiene products, some medications, and items for letter writing and clothing can also be found. Things like a toothbrush, toothpaste, and dental floss are not provided for you in jail. Most also do not allow razors or shaving items, so beards and facial hair are common in jail. Most of your hygiene items must be purchased through the commissary, or you can go without them.

Certain medications can also be purchased. Tylenol, fungal creams, antibiotic ointment, and talc are a few of the most basic items. Most other medical creams, medication, and ointments are available only by going to sick call to see a doctor or nurse. The costs will vary depending on the jail where you are housed, but most will cost you at least $10 for the visit and the medications. You also must wait for long periods of time to see the doctor or nurse and then wait for the medication to be ordered and delivered.

Various clothing items are also available for purchase. Because most jails lack heat in the winter months and air conditioning in the summer, certain clothing options become very helpful: thermal tops and bottoms in the winter months and shorts and T-shirts during the summer. Often, jails also lack the sizes you need, so you are given whatever they have available. Once, after returning from prison to jail to attend a court appearance, I was given underwear that was three sizes too big! It was all they had to give me, but impossible for me to wear. So, at times commissary is the only option to get clothing that fits. Everything from socks to underwear, T-shirts, and thermals, to sweatshirts and shower shoes are offered. Because jails often run out of clothing and bedding, it is important to get the clothing you need when you first arrive.

There are also miscellaneous items like stamps, paper, envelopes, and other materials for legal work that can be purchased. In order to contact people from jail, letters or phone calls are your best options. If you want to use the phone to contact your loved ones, money can be transferred from your commissary to your phone account to make phone calls. Though calls can be very expensive, ranging from $3.50 up to $15 for one fifteen-minute call, they are the quickest and easiest way to contact those you need to speak with.

COMMISSARY CAUTIONS

The commissary is a great benefit to have while in jail, but with the good also comes the challenges. Many use the commissary in jail, but many more do not. If you use it, people will approach you to borrow or just have you give them things. You must be careful and use your judgment when sharing items with others to prevent a perception that you will share anything with anyone. Though it garners some goodwill to be generous with what you have, others will take advantage and perceive your kindness as a weakness and will try to coerce you into giving up all of your commissaries by threatening to harm you if you do not comply.

There is also a potential danger from gangs who look to exploit people by stealing their commissary and taking advantage of those who are weak or intimidated by them. Because commissary is the currency in jail, many will want to take advantage if they can to use it for their own purposes. You can avoid becoming a target by not ordering large amounts at one time, keeping your items hidden, and not letting people know what you have. Discretion can help you maintain a low profile and avoid getting items taken or being exploited by others.

Chapter 7

Judicial Procedures and Hearings

N ow that you have a basic understanding of what will happen when you are arrested and booked into jail, your journey through the judicial process begins. These early steps in the criminal procedures can feel overwhelming to someone experiencing this for the first time. But with knowledge and a basic understanding of how the process works, you can navigate these steps and protect your rights and due process along the way.

ARRAIGNMENT

The arraignment is the first step in your criminal procedures. This is your opportunity to have the charges read to you by the judge if you choose. Depending on the severity of your charges, you may be able, at this point, to receive a bond or be released by signing paperwork that says you will show up for all court appearances. If you have felony charges that are more severe, you will have to be seen in Superior Court. You will most likely have a bond hearing to allow the judge an opportunity to hear arguments for or against you receiving a bond.

BOND HEARING

If you have felony charges and your first court appearance is in front of a Superior Court judge, that judge will set a date for a bond hearing, usually within a week of your arrest. At this phase of the process, several factors are considered in your bond hearing. The first is your criminal history. If you have been arrested before or had similar offenses, these may factor into the judge's decision to grant a bond. Judges also consider the severity of the charges, the potential danger to the public, and whether the person is a flight risk. Generally, if the person accused of a crime has a job, owns a home, has a family, and is well-established in the community with no previous criminal history, these things should help mitigate some of the concerns that judges may have in giving a bond. This is not always the case, however.

When I went for my bond hearing, I was employed, had lived in the state for 16 years, had owned three homes in the state, and had a wife and family. I also had no criminal history whatsoever and not so much as a traffic ticket in 38 years! However, when it came time for the judge to rule on my bond motion, she denied my bond. Without providing any explanation about why my bond was denied, she simply said no. In most cases, the judge will at least give a reason for denying a bond, but in my case, no reason was given. Others I have spoken with who have similar charges to mine received bonds. One of those awaiting trial for three years, working and living his life before being convicted. There is no way to predict how a bond hearing will go, but having a competent attorney, no criminal history, and stability in your job, home, and family give you the best chance of getting a bond.

OTHER FACTORS CONSIDERED FOR BOND

Another consideration that judges are tasked with is the propensity of the accused to commit other crimes should that person be released on bond. Judges must weigh whether someone they allow out on bond would continue to commit crimes while awaiting the outcome of the criminal case. Again, the factors already considered are once again a part of the equation, as well as any other factors the prosecution may present to the judge at the hearing. If it was a violent crime where the victim received bodily harm, the judge may reject the bond for fear of reprisals by the accused should that person be released. Also, if there is strong evidence other crimes may be committed if they release an individual, that may prevent that person from receiving a bond.

When considering these other factors in light of my case, I was arrested eight months after the alleged incident took place. The prosecution was in possession of the medical records, surveillance footage, and witness statements and had fully investigated the claim. So, based on its investigation, they had no evidence to present that would indicate I was a danger to the community or a flight risk. Instead, they argued that because I used an alias, it somehow made me a flight risk, and the judge agreed. As absurd as I thought it was at the time, I also came to realize the state I was convicted in has a long history of misguided prosecutions and wrongful convictions, so it was not a surprise to most to hear how they dealt with me in my bond hearing.

What was surprising to many is that all of the defendants who were with me that day in court did receive a bond from the same judge. These men, while awaiting their bond hearings, were reciting their crimes to each other that they, in actuality, were guilty of and were arrested for. They all laughed as they told how they had gotten off for many other crimes in the past and described their lengthy prison records and how they would again escape justice. I was horrified as I listened to them describe how they had murdered, raped, robbed, and assaulted people and still felt confident they would get a bond and beat their current cases. They had in the past, and they felt confident they could once again. After talking to my attorney and others in jail, I thought there was no way that they would get a bond based on the factors that the judge was to consider. However, when it came time for their hearings, each one came back with a bond, except for me.

This was the first time that I started to wonder whether all the things I believed growing up were true. I used to believe that justice was always served in the criminal cases I saw on television and that if you were arrested, you were guilty. But now I was beginning to question for the first time in my life whether the system was really fair or just. I felt in my case, it was not, especially after my bond hearing and knowing what I did about those who received a bond that day. Justice was not served in fairness or by the letter of the law that day.

FORMAL CHARGES/INDICTMENT

The next step in your criminal proceedings is the formal charges that are made against you. Each state has its own set of proceedings to accomplish this, but in my state, it was through a grand Jury indictment. Grand juries are convened behind closed doors and not open to the public. Only the prosecution is allowed to present evidence during this hearing. I was not able to attend this procedure, and later, I learned they used false testimony directly from the accuser and one of the prosecutors in order to secure an indictment. The accuser testified to various physical injuries that allegedly occurred the night in question. The prosecutor then testified that they had not yet received the medical records from the hospital to substantiate the accuser's claims. Both of those testimonies were false and not at all in harmony with the medical records or facts that were available at the time of the hearing.

Later, in a separate hearing, the prosecutor was put on the stand to explain how she was not aware that they had been in possession of the medical records for almost eight months prior to the grand Jury proceedings. She denied any knowledge of the medical records availability at the time of her testimony, and we had no way to prove she was lying at that time. However, when we received the discovery from the prosecution, the date the paperwork was received from the hospital was on each page, thereby proving we were right and the prosecution had lied to cover up for the victim's false testimony during the grand Jury indictment. We were first made aware of what was testified to during the grand Jury hearings by the prosecution, which indicated the victim had given testimony over the phone of alleged injuries sustained that night. Later, after receiving the medical records that showed the accuser had no injuries from that night, we tried to get the indictment thrown out, but the judge allowed for it to stand because we could not prove the prosecution's attorney was aware of the records at the time of her testimony. However, it would be extremely unlikely that an attorney working on the case for over eight months would not be aware that the medical records were in their possession. It is far more likely that she was lying to cover for the victim, who had lied about her pretended injuries and even admitted to doing so in text messages to her friends. So, in addition to my judge's questionable ruling on my bond request, I now had the prosecution lying about the medical records and what they knew in order to secure an indictment. This was further evidence that the prosecution was not interested in the truth, only in getting a conviction.

PLEA AGREEMENTS

After the indictment, then there is a period of time when you can either negotiate a plea agreement with the prosecution or prepare to go to trial. Approximately 90 percent of all criminal cases end in a plea deal, with only 10 percent going to trial. Plea agreements give an accused person a way to negotiate a lesser charge or take less time in exchange for their guilty plea. If you are indeed guilty, a plea deal is the best option to take to limit your time in prison. However, if you are innocent, you may want to take your case all the way to trial. Though most attorneys will tell you to take a deal, you also need to keep in mind they are not always looking out for you as much as they are not wanting to take the time and effort to prepare to go to trial. Because most are paid upfront for their services, it doesn't matter to them if you go to trial or take a plea. It is in their best interest to settle the case and not have to go to trial. But for the accused, you give up most of your rights to fight your case when you take a plea deal. You must make the decision whether to take a deal very carefully. The following are some tips on how to come to that decision and the rights that you have and can take advantage of in order to make an informed decision.

RIGHT TO SEE EVIDENCE

It is your due process right to review the evidence that the prosecution has against you. You will want to request that your attorney bring all of your discovery evidence to you so that you can evaluate and be prepared for what will be used against you in court. When I went through this process, I asked my attorney if I could see the discovery evidence the prosecution had given to him. However, he would not bring it to me because he claimed there was too much to bring—which was a blatant lie. When the trial started, there were a few boxes of evidence, but nothing like what he described, and there was no reason he could not have brought it for me to review. Had I done so, I would have been made aware of incriminating evidence against the accuser that was kept from my knowledge until the trial. Only after the trial started was I aware that the prosecution had "cut a deal" with my attorney to have the evidence that would have exonerated me excluded from being used. I came across the evidence only as I was reading text messages from the accuser's phone that indicated she had made up the story and specific details because the police did not believe her. She also used profanity to describe the detectives working on the case and how she lied to them to get them to pursue it. She also complained about how they kept insisting there was no evidence a crime had been committed, so she continued to lie and make increasingly ridiculous claims to get the police to take her seriously. Ultimately, they did, even though they had proof she had been lying all along.

I found my attorney's response to why we were not questioning the witness about her admissions in her texts very disturbing. Several weeks before the trial, he told me that the prosecutor had called him and asked to have the text messages off-limits during the trial. He said the 1,400 text messages were irrelevant to the case. My attorney later admitted he did not carefully read through the texts and agreed to exclude them. He did so without consulting me or reading the texts to see if there was anything incriminating in them or if the prosecution was trying to hide evidence that could be used against their accuser. I was concerned that my attorney was not acting in my best interest and had made a deal with the prosecution. Looking back now, I believe that was indeed the case. I feel very confident he was working with them because he was a dishonest man who extorted money from us, even during the trial, lied about his experience, and did not prepare for the trial. Working with them made his job easy and did not require him to do any work. In addition, he made a mistake that a first-year law student would not make, and that was to agree to exclude evidence that he never looked through to determine its value or to find if there was anything the prosecution was trying to keep from coming to light. Those texts were a big key to proving my innocence. I do not believe an attorney with 30 years of experience would make that mistake. I believe he knew and did it to capitulate to the prosecution. That is why you cannot rely on an attorney to be the only one who looks through the evidence and makes decisions for you without your consent. Your attorney works for you, and if the attorney refuses to allow you to see all of the evidence against you, it is time to find another attorney. The fact is a good attorney will work with you and help you, not hide evidence from you or make arbitrary decisions without consulting you first. Because I was not aware of the texts and the judicial process and trusted that my attorney I paid good money to was working for me, I forfeited many opportunities to help myself by not demanding to see and review the evidence against me and by not being aware of my rights at the time.

PRETRIAL MOTIONS

Depending on the complexity of your case, there might be many pretrial motions to determine what evidence is admissible, who will testify, and when your trial will take place. Before my trial, I had several hearings to determine if certain people who had nothing to do with my case could testify against me and what their testimonies would be. The prosecution, in an effort to slander and prejudice the jury against me, found people who would testify and give false statements that gave the jury a false impression about who I was as a person. The detectives on the case lied about what I did, who I was, and what happened the night in question to those who ended up testifying in order to secure their testimony. They deliberately misled their witnesses by saying I may not get convicted. Had they not deliberately misled their witnesses, I may not have been convicted, and other people would not have been hurt if they didn't testify. These lies and deceitful tactics are used to manipulate people into testifying against those who are often innocent of the charges against them but are made to believe otherwise after speaking to the police. It is absolutely hypocritical and wrong that law enforcement is allowed to lie, manipulate, and twist the facts to suit their purposes. But if a defendant were to lie, that person would be prosecuted. How does the criminal justice system, which is supposed to be a just and fair process, allow for such inconsistencies and unfairness? Sadly, this is the state of our justice system today in many states and cities across the country. It is not limited to one area of the country, as I have spoken to people who have served time in many cities and states, and the same things are happening all over the country.

TRANSCRIPTS FROM HEARINGS

Each hearing will have a transcript that can be requested and reviewed before the trial. It is important to have copies of each transcript to review because, often, testimony changes and details emerge between the time of the hearings and the trial. One of the hearings I had gave me the opportunity to hear from the alleged victim in my case and her testimony of the events of the night in question. She gave a vivid description of events that she said she could remember from that night and many things that I was not aware of that took place after we parted ways for the evening. Having that information was critical for the trial because as a result of her testimony, we were able to have some tests done on clothing she wore that night that enabled us to impeach her testimony at trial. Because her testimony was on the record, and we had the transcripts to show how her testimony had changed from the previous hearing to the actual trial, we were able to show her deception. Transcripts enable you to detect deception and prepare your defense for trial.

DON'T RELY SOLELY ON YOUR ATTORNEY

Each case differs in complexity and scope; but no matter how many hearings you have as you prepare for trial, it is vital to understand what the purpose is for the hearings and to be prepared for each one. Do not depend on your attorney to inform you of all the information or allow them to just handle things for you. It is your life and your freedom at stake. You must do all you can to be aware of the laws where you live. If necessary, go to the law library that each jail provides to become familiar with the laws and processes in the jurisdiction where you are incarcerated. By doing your homework and not relying solely on your attorney, you can help prevent avoidable mistakes and protect yourself and your rights throughout the entire process.

Chapter 8

Preparing For Trial

THE DECISION T0 GO TO TRIAL

Making the decision to go to trial should be carefully thought out and all the options weighed. If you are innocent, going to trial makes sense if you feel you can prove your innocence to a jury. This also preserves your right to appeal the verdict if found guilty. If you are guilty, you should take whatever deal is being offered by the prosecution; otherwise, there is a very good chance going to trial will only add time to your sentence. Keep in mind that most cases that go to trial end in a conviction. In fact, only 10 percent of all cases go to trial, and of those, only 2 percent are exonerated. That does not mean that only 2 percent of people who go to trial are innocent; it just means that the prosecution has more resources and money to use against those who took their cases to trial. For example, because the state pays for the prosecution, they have more money for witnesses, more lawyers to work on cases, investigators to track down leads, and also the police to gather evidence for them. Conversely, defense lawyers are expensive, require additional money for experts and investigators, and even more money if additional legal help is necessary. Hiring a good defense attorney will cost the average person between 50,000 to 100,000 dollars or more. Each attorney I spoke to regarding my case wanted in this price range or more to defend me. The prosecution also enlists the media to help sway public opinion against you in a trial, so you are up against formidable odds. However, with a good attorney, the truth, and the right preparation, you can beat the odds. The following are some things I have learned that may help you prepare for your trial.

REVIEWING THE EVIDENCE AGAINST YOU

This is a critical first step for anyone going to trial: do not assume that your attorney will just handle it or that he or she is telling you everything. Because this is your case and your life, you need to be a part of the process every step of the way. Also, because you know what happened better than anyone else, you can provide key information based on the evidence that you have to help prepare for any arguments the prosecution may make against you. My case had over 1,400 text messages that my attorney did not make the effort to read. He then made a deal with the prosecution to exclude them from the trial without asking me first. He also refused to bring in the evidence so I could review everything because he said there was simply too much evidence to bring in. In the end, I realized he had lied about all of these things, and in large part, he was the reason why I was convicted. Had I been able to review the texts and other evidence prior to my trial, I would have found key evidence that ended up never being presented that could have easily exonerated me. Do not make that same mistake by not being involved in the process. Demand to see all the evidence, make your attorney review it with you, go over the strategy, and make sure anything your attorney does is approved with you first.

LAW LIBRARY AND INTERNET RESOURCES

Every state has different laws, statutes, and processes for trial. While you are awaiting your trial, it is important to review the laws and statutes that are applicable to your case. Become familiar with the legal process in your state, and be prepared for each step as you go. Knowledge is power and could help keep you from a lengthy prison term. Knowing what your rights are, what to expect, and how the process works helps you to avoid feeling overwhelmed and afraid. Instead, it enables you to pay attention and ensure your rights are preserved and protected. Do not be afraid to question things if you feel something is not right. Ask the judge or your attorney to explain things if you don't understand what is happening. The law library is a helpful tool if you are in jail; or if you are awaiting trial on bond, you can use the vast resources found online to research your specific charges and the process that your jurisdiction follows. Preparation is key to not allowing the system or your attorney to take advantage due to your ignorance. When I went to trial, I was like a deer in the headlights, unsure of what to expect and had no idea what my rights were or the steps in the process. I was scared and completely dependent on my attorney for everything, and he failed me miserably. Had I done my research, I could have kept him from sabotaging my case and, consequently, my life. But I did not, and now I can only warn others not to make the same mistakes. Do your homework! No matter how much money you pay your attorney or how much they reassure you that they are doing all they can, do not rely on your attorney alone. Do all you can to know the laws, statutes, and process. This will give you the ability to know what to do and how to do it and may end up saving your life and keeping you out of prison.

WITNESSES AND EVIDENCE

Many cases nowadays hinge on eyewitness testimony or witnesses who are used to corroborate the story being presented at trial. It is important to have those who can testify to your innocence be available to testify on your behalf. Conversely, you need also to be aware of who is testifying against you and be prepared to question them when they take the stand. To do these things, you need to have your attorney or an investigator track down the people who can help you and get them to testify. Provide all names and contacts to your attorney and ensure he contacts them and gets their side of the story. Also, any video, emails, texts, and interviews done by the police and turned over during discovery needs to be carefully reviewed. Any evidence that you know of that can prove your innocence should be given to your attorney to use in your defense. Be honest and forthcoming because any surprises can be devastating to your case.

DISCOVERY AND EVIDENCE

In the course of preparing for your trial, the prosecution is required to turn over all evidence collected during its investigation. This is another critical area you need to pay attention to. Often, the prosecution will fail to turn over key evidence or omit certain things that may prove to be damaging to their case. It is important that your attorney be thorough in their own investigation of the facts, know what the prosecution has, and make sure it is given when you receive the discovery for your case. When I went to trial, key evidence was withheld from us regarding medical information that was only discovered after the trial and during my appellate case. This information directly refuted some of the testimony given at my trial that turned out to be false. Having this information withheld, I feel, was done deliberately to hide evidence from the jury, just as they did with the text messages. This is why having a good attorney is vital to getting all relevant information and evidence to defend you. Making sure your attorney questions and files complaints if the evidence is not turned over in a timely fashion will also help to ensure the prosecution plays by the rules and turns over all of the evidence before your trial.

MENTAL PREPARATIONS

Prepare all you can with the physical evidence and prepare yourself emotionally for what is about to take place. Going to trial is scary and feels overwhelming. People look at you differently and already have preconceived notions about your guilt or innocence. It is very difficult to handle all those moments of emotions and stress. Though no amount of preparation will ever fully prepare you for that time, some things may help you manage those feelings and assist you to focus instead on your defense and what is happening in the courtroom. One of the best ways to prepare emotionally is to be prepared in every way for your trial. By knowing and reviewing all the evidence and witness testimony, you alleviate some of the concerns of the unknown. When you are prepared, you feel less anxiety and stress. However, even advanced preparation does not remove all of your angst. It will help to know you are ready and prepared to defend yourself against whatever the prosecution throws at you.

PRAYER AND MEDITATION

If you are a religious person like me, prayer was a needful thing in the days leading up to my trial. I spent a lot of time praying for the truth to come out and for the court to render a fair and just verdict. No matter where you are in the days leading up to your trial, you will feel the stress and anxiety levels increase, and you will need to have time to reflect, pray, and meditate to help reduce the stress and anxiety that you will inevitably feel as your freedom hangs in the balance. Though my trial did not turn out at all like I thought it would, I did feel at peace because I knew I was innocent of the charges and that it was the system, not me, that was in the wrong.

Chapter 9

Trial

MENTAL PREPARATION

T he trial is one of the most difficult and challenging aspects of the criminal process. For those who are innocent, the stress and anxiety that come with defending against false allegations feels, at times, overwhelming. The reasons for this vary but are mainly due to how a person is treated during this process. It starts with the prosecution doing everything possible to demonize and dehumanize those they prosecute in the eyes of all who are present and in the media. Those who take their case to trial must be prepared to get sideways looks from those seated in the courtroom. Many in the courtroom will also assume those accused are already guilty, make comments, and look at them with disgust each time they enter and exit during the trial. For these and many other reasons, the courtroom is a very intimidating place. Those who stand accused must be ready for the stress and anxiety that comes with defending yourself and your life against those determined to see you go to prison.

For those with "high-profile" cases, meaning cases covered by the news media, there is added scrutiny and persecution. With the whole world connected by social media, news about "high-profile" cases is widely known by many people. This means those on the jury for those cases will most likely know what the media has said about the case. Though they are asked if they have seen or heard anything about the cases in the news or on the internet, many will claim they have not heard about it to prevent being removed from the jury pool. Those who admit to hearing about the cases are removed due to possible prejudice about the case. This adds another hurdle to overcome for those cases with much media scrutiny. It is exactly why many "high-profile" cases are hard to win; in society today, you are guilty until proven innocent, not the other way around. My case was deemed "high profile" because the district attorney's office had my story on the news within hours of my arrest. I had no idea why I was deemed so important to them, but I was. This media coverage made it harder for me in jail because people everywhere were familiar with my case. Jail guards would often make ignorant comments that were demeaning, and inmates were cruel and poked fun at me in inappropriate ways. Because the story portrayed in the media was untrue, people falsely perceived who I was and what had happened. I was being portrayed as something I was not, and the reactions and comments made by the jail guards and inmates who did not know foreshadowed what many in my jury pool expressed when we were tasked with picking a jury. Jail is difficult enough without the added stress that going to trial brings. But if your case is also covered in the media, it makes it much harder to get a fair trial and to find impartial jurors who do not have their minds made up before your trial even begins. Though you have many months to prepare for trial, nothing can get you ready for what you will experience in the courtroom or the physical and mental toll it takes on your body. Based on my own experience, I believe going to trial is one of the most difficult experiences a person can go through.

PROCESS WITHOUT BOND

Many who are awaiting trial are fortunate to get a bond, but for those who do not, the process is grueling and painful. The morning trial begins, those in jail are awakened as early as 3 am to get their breakfast. Then, a short time later, they are told to prepare to go to court. Around 5 am, they are then taken to a holding cell for those going to court that day. Once all inmates are accounted for, each is shackled and escorted out to a bus and transported to the courthouse. The handcuffs and ankle chains are usually tight and often cut into the skin on ankles and wrists. Once inmates arrive at the courthouse, they are escorted off the bus and taken to a holding area where each name is read, and then prisoners are taken to another holding cell after passing through a metal detector. These cells in the courthouse are usually very cold and damp and often smell of urine and mold. Once all are inside, bologna sandwiches are given to each inmate with a pint of milk or orange juice. That is all the food each inmate receives until the inmate returns from court that evening. This process varies depending on the state or county where you are locked up, but most have very similar procedures and processes.

A short time later, a docket is read for each of the judges that day. Each inmate is then taken to a holding cell on the corresponding floor of the judge they are there to see. There, inmates must wait until their turn to go before the judge. This is also the time they will change into a suit that either their family brings from home or a court-provided one when necessary. After changing, you then await word from the judge to be brought into the courtroom. Then, the trial begins.

JURY SELECTION

The first step that happens when your trial starts is to have the charges read aloud to the potential jurors. While sitting in the courtroom with those who will decide your fate, the judge has the charges read to the potential jurors. Each charge is described in detail, and the meaning of the charge is explained. During this process of my trial, it was very difficult to hear the charges they alleged against me. As I looked around at the people assembled in the room, I felt that it also had a very negative effect on them. My fears were confirmed as we spoke to potential jurors about their ability to be impartial and listen to all the evidence before deciding my guilt or innocence. Many said they were disgusted and could not even look at me based solely on the charges that were read in court that morning.

Sadly, this is how many people feel nowadays before trials even begin. Many will think the accused is guilty before any of the evidence is presented. The current criminal process ensures that guilt is already assumed, and the accused person now has to prove his or her innocence rather than innocent until proven guilty. Though the justice system claims that it considers a person innocent until proven otherwise, today, it treats an accused person as guilty until proven innocent, and the judicial process that is followed helps ensure jurors feel the same.

When selecting a jury, each side has the opportunity to select those jurors they feel will be sympathetic to their case. However, each side also has the ability to object to and remove up to eight jurors. Once each side has selected the people they want and have no more objections, the jury is set, and the trial can begin.

OPENING STATEMENTS

Opening statements at a trial are simply an opportunity for each side to state its version of the events, what they want the jury to focus on, and what they believe they can prove to the jury. These statements do not have to be factual, based on evidence, or even truthful. This applies to both opening and closing statements. Neither side has to be based on facts, evidence, or the truth. They can simply be whatever each side wants them to be. I quickly learned in court that much of what takes place in the courtroom has little to do with the truth, facts, or evidence. Instead, courtrooms are more about who can tell the best story and get a jury to believe their version of the events. If courtrooms were more about truth and innocence, I would not be in prison today.

The prosecution begins with its opening statement. Those prosecuting my case had a very well-prepared PowerPoint presentation that outlined a very compelling but false story. Though most of it was not based on facts, evidence, or testimony, it did present the jury with a story that could explain what happened the night in question. My attorney, meanwhile, was writing his opening statement on a pad of notebook paper while the prosecution made its opening remarks. I was immediately concerned by this apparent lack of preparation but thought that maybe he just did not like to write things down or that he already knew what he wanted to say. I was wrong.

After the prosecution was done, my attorney got up and made some simple statements about things we could prove based on the evidence and then sat down. There was no attempt made to explain to the jury what happened that night, any explanation for the things that took place, or even a theory on why things happened the way they did. It was embarrassing for me and for him. I heard people laughing and mocking him as he sat down. I had no idea at that time that the entire trial would be exactly the same.

The opening statements are an opportunity to help the jury understand your side of the story and to highlight the points you are trying to make. It is important that your attorney is well-prepared to tell your side of the story, what you are planning to prove, and the reason why you should not be convicted. Before your trial begins, you should have your attorney share with you what he plans to tell the jurors to ensure you feel comfortable with his approach and that he includes all pertinent information. Do not assume anything when it comes to your attorney and his or her preparation for trial. This is your life on the line, not theirs. Therefore, it is imperative that you are fully invested in all that your attorney does and says. You have the right to be a part of the strategy and planning for your case. So make sure you speak to your attorney and know ahead of time how that person is going to present your case.

PRESENTING WITNESSES AND EVIDENCE

After the opening statements by both sides, the prosecution then begins to present its case by calling witnesses and presenting evidence. This phase of the trial can last days or even weeks, depending on the complexity of the case. This is an important time to pay attention to what the witnesses are saying and to write down anything that is said that contradicts what really happened or what might have been said in a previous hearing. Often, witness testimony changes over time based on evidence that comes to light or other witnesses' testimonies. This was the case in my trial. Between the last motions hearing we had and the trial, we opted to have a key piece of evidence tested to prove one aspect of our case. When the evidence came back in our favor, proving what I had been saying from the start, it forced the accuser to change her story to account for this new evidence, thus proving her previous statements were false. However, because of my attorney's incompetence, lack of preparation, and insufficient knowledge of current laws, he fumbled away an opportunity to properly impeach the witness. To impeach a witness means to prove they are lying.

Once the prosecution has presented all its evidence and witness testimony, the defense is then allowed to present its case. It is important to ensure your attorney tells the jury your version of the events, presents all evidence that proves your story to be true, and refutes any evidence and testimony that was given by the prosecution that is false or misleading. Expert witnesses are also helpful but must be carefully vetted to make sure they are credible and legitimate in their field of expertise.

My attorney had numerous opportunities to impeach witnesses but lacked the preparation and knowledge to do so. This is the reason why it is important to be aware of the statements witnesses have given in hearings prior to the trial, and also during the proceedings. Attorneys are generally good at finding these inconsistencies, but they also miss things, too. Being aware and ensuring your attorney attacks any statements made by the witnesses that contradict previous statements or are false in general will help impeach witness testimony and discredit them. If the jury does not believe the testimony given, it gives them probable cause to find the accused innocent of the charges.

My attorney hired several experts for my case. One of those experts gave a sworn affidavit in my favor without actually looking at the evidence first. So when he came to court, the prosecution was able to get him to admit he gave the sworn affidavit prior to reviewing the evidence and, therefore, rendered his testimony useless. The other expert we hired to work the audio/visual aspect of my case died of a massive heart attack the night before my trial started. When the judge declined to give us time to find another expert, we had to find someone last minute. But when he was not able to get it working properly within the timeframe the judge arbitrarily set, none of that evidence was seen by the jury either.

My attorney had numerous opportunities to impeach witnesses but lacked the preparation and knowledge to do so. This is the reason why it is important to be aware of the statements witnesses have given in hearings prior to the trial, and also during the proceedings. Attorneys are generally good at finding these inconsistencies, but they also miss things, too. Being aware and ensuring your attorney attacks any statements made by the witnesses that contradict previous statements or are false in general will help impeach witness testimony and discredit them. If the jury does not believe the testimony given, it gives them probable cause to find the accused innocent of the charges.

The last and most important evidence that proved my innocence came from the accuser directly in the form of texts. However, the jury never saw those texts because my attorney made a deal with the prosecutor to disregard the 1,400 text messages from the accuser's phone that included her confession that the story was a lie, that she made up the allegations, and many other things she lied about during the trial. But because my attorney made a deal behind my back, and without looking through the texts first, none of those things were told to the jury. Before your trial begins, you should have your attorney share with you what he or she plans to tell the jurors to ensure you feel comfortable with the approach and that the attorney includes all pertinent information. Do not assume anything when it comes to your attorney and that person's preparation for trial. Remember, it is your life to lose, so take ownership of it and make sure you have an attorney who is working for you and not against you.

CLOSING STATEMENTS/JURY INSTRUCTIONS

After the defense rests its case, the judge will then ask the prosecution in what order they would like to give their closing statements. The prosecution gets to decide if they go first or last. Often, the prosecution will defer to go last to be able to refute whatever is said by the defense. This also allows the prosecution to have the final say in the trial without the defense being able to challenge what is said. This was the case in my trial. In fact, the prosecution waited until its closing statements to assert ridiculous claims that were never mentioned during the trial. Statements do not have to be factual or based on evidence; they could make up any accusations they wanted to leave the jury feeling like I had to be guilty because we had nothing to refute their claims. Without an opportunity to refute these false allegations, once again, the process leaves the defendants at a disadvantage. The last things the jury hears are often the lies that the prosecution alleges with no evidence or truth to substantiate their claims.

After closing statements, the judge will then give any relevant jury instructions that the defense and prosecution deem necessary for the jury to ensure they have all they need to return a fair and correct verdict. Jury instructions are important; if not instructed correctly, this could be a violation of the due process of the accused. It is important to make sure the judge gives the jury all relevant jury instructions and that those instructions are followed. If not followed, that can be grounds for an appeal if the accused is found guilty.

VERDICT/SENTENCE

Once the jury reaches a verdict, the accused and jury are then brought back into the courtroom, and the verdict is read aloud in the court. For the accused, this is a very emotional moment. Though many do not always express a lot of emotions when the verdict is read, it is often due to the initial shock and the realization of what has just happened. For those who are found innocent, immediate relief and tears are evident right away. Conversely, if found guilty, the shock and the realization that you are going to prison have almost a numbing effect initially. You find yourself not knowing how to feel and completely in shock about what just happened. Often, the news media will comment that those found guilty are emotionless or unfeeling when convicted. That is as far from the truth as it can be. The truth is you try as hard as you can to control your emotions in the moment, knowing that if you break down right then and there, you might not get control of your emotions for a long time afterward. With family, news media, and others looking on, many try to contain those feelings until later in their jail cell, where they can be alone with their thoughts and feelings.

No matter if you are found innocent or guilty, the emotional strain and physical stress a person goes through when on trial is enormous. So, when it comes to an end, an emotional release is inevitable. For me, the night I was convicted was one of the hardest of my life. I cried myself to sleep that night, wondering how I would survive in prison, what would happen to my family, and if my life as I knew it was now over. I had to face the reality of going to prison and begin to prepare myself for a world I hoped I would never be a part of. For those who go to prison for the first time, not knowing what to expect is the hardest part. So now I will help you know how to prepare for prison if that is your verdict.

Chapter 10

Diagnostic Testing

TESTING AND EVALUATION

After trial, those who are convicted go back to county jail to await being transferred to a diagnostic prison facility. Most states send newly convicted inmates to a facility initially to evaluate their mental, physical, and emotional health before assigning them to a permanent facility. This process usually takes between two to four weeks. However, if there are any outstanding medical conditions or problems that arise, this process can be delayed until treatment can be given.

During the diagnostic process, inmates are tested for sexually transmitted diseases and other health-related issues and competency in the basics of math, English, reading, and spelling. Inmates are also asked if they are affiliated with any gangs or other organizations and checked for tattoos. Depending on the gang affiliations and the crimes committed, these factors often lead to higher security designations for affiliated inmates. Then, based on all of the evaluations, combined with the test results and mental and physical evaluations, inmates are then assigned to a permanent facility to serve their sentence.

The testing and evaluation aspect lasts only about a week. The rest of the time you spend awaiting transfer to your new facility and praying it is a place that has decent food, is safe, and has classes and other activities to pass the time in productive ways. The diagnostic prison I went to was the worst experience of my life.

After the week of testing and evaluation, I spent the next four weeks trying to learn and survive my first taste of prison life. It was not like anything I had ever seen in a movie or experienced before. It was worse than I ever imagined it could be. The food was meager and tasteless and often had insects or other foreign objects in it. The cellhouses were cold, overrun with rats and cockroaches, and the scent of burning paper and smoke made me nauseous.

VIOLENT ENVIRONMENT

Being completely out of my element when I first arrived, I had to learn how to carry myself in a very violent and volatile environment. My first night in the diagnostic facility had me on edge because I was told not to unpack until I was given permission to do so by the leader of a gang whose cell I was assigned to. I did not know at the time that the gangs controlled the cells in the cellblock I was housed in. If you were a civilian or someone not affiliated with a gang, you were kicked out of the cell or charged a fee to stay there. When I arrived in the cell I was assigned to, it was under Muslim control. I was told I would be meeting the head man of the Muslims, and he would decide if I stayed in the cell or not. After meeting me, he decided I could stay, but that was just the beginning of a series of events that quickly awakened me to the realities of prison life.

Within days after my arrival, I witnessed men being beaten, stabbed, and thrown out of cells because they would not pay extortion fees to gangs. I saw a gang war in the showers of over 40 inmates at one time. I saw gang initiations where the person being initiated had to fight the entire gang at once and was beaten until he could not stand up anymore. I also saw people beaten who were weak and could not defend themselves because of mental or physical deformities. I learned that prison is unforgiving and that the strong prey upon the weak and handicapped.

Much like animals in the wild, if other inmates sense weakness or vulnerability, many will use that to take advantage or abuse those whom they feel they can bully or intimidate. The only way to prevent that is to stand up to those who try to bully you and not allow them to intimidate you, or it will never stop. I also figured out that fighting does not solve the problem either. Fighting just leads to more fighting, and then people get seriously injured or killed. I saw this firsthand as a man was badly injured and beaten in front of my cellmate and me. On that occasion, a knife was brandished, and I feared I would see this man get stabbed right in front of me. Thankfully, the knife was never used. Though these first few weeks in prison were traumatizing and difficult to endure, they did help prepare me for what I would experience routinely in prison life.

While at this facility where I am permanently housed, cell houses are used to house the most violent elements who have demonstrated an inability to control themselves or keep from harming others. Because prison life is difficult, especially for those without family or support, many join gangs for protection and for help to get food and other necessities while incarcerated. The flip side is you are also obligated to do as you are told to do, even if that means participating in things that will ultimately get you more time in prison or perhaps prevent you from leaving. I will discuss gangs further as I speak about different aspects of prison; however, for now, it is important to know that gangs are a huge part of prison life and one that you have to be familiar with in order to safely navigate a prison sentence.

TRANSFERS

At the end of your time at the diagnostic facility, you will receive what is designated as a "call out" when your time comes to transfer. This comes the morning you are being transferred to your permanent facility. That day could not come fast enough for me as I was already feeling like I could never survive my sentence in prison if it were going to be like the diagnostic facility. To my relief, I was assigned to a private prison that had better food and a better environment, according to those who were familiar with the camp. Anything was better than where I had been, so I was more than ready to leave. However, I need to explain in the next chapter the difference between a private prison and a state-run facility.

Chapter 11

Private vs. State

W hile awaiting your permanent camp assignment, many inmates will tell you stories and give you insights into what you will experience at a state or private facility. For most, private prisons are the preferred destination for many prisoners because of what they offer that state institutions do not. Private prisons have the reputation of providing better food, safer housing, air conditioning, more educational opportunities, and a more laid-back environment. State facilities are notorious for giving very little food, no air conditioning, more violent and volatile facilities, fewer correctional officers, more rigid inspections, and dirtier and more unsanitary dorms, according to those who have been to state facilities.

STATE PRISONS

State prisons in the state I am incarcerated in are constantly in the news for various reasons. In a recent news article, it told the story of a guard who worked at a state-run facility that was plagued by understaffing, violence, and poor working conditions. In the article, the guard describes how he worked 16-hour days five days a week in a building by himself that housed over 600 inmates. As he worked there, he had urine and feces thrown in his face and mattresses set on fire to protest the poor conditions in the prison. He worked there for about a year before eventually leaving because of the poor working conditions, low pay, and the lack of staffing. However, the problems were not just at that facility; according to the article, prison facilities, in general, had lost, on average, between 30 to 50 percent of their staff since the pandemic. Even with higher starting wages and better benefits, most state facilities remain woefully understaffed and volatile.

Inmates coming from state facilities relate stories of people dying and the bodies not being found for several days. One inmate told of another who was murdered, wrapped in a sheet, and put under his bunk. Only the stench of his decaying body led to him being discovered almost a week later. Prisons are required to do standing counts five times per day, where inmates stand in front of their bunks to be accounted for. The fact that it was almost a week before the body was found demonstrates how officers were not doing their job and conducting inaccurate counts.

Counts are done so that if an inmate were to escape or go missing, staff would know because the count would be off. If the counts are not done correctly, someone could escape or be killed, and it could be many days until the body is discovered. Understaffing has left prisons vulnerable to errors like these because of the overworked staff and lack of security.

This same article also interviewed women who were housed in state prisons, and they said they were often understaffed, not given their personal hygiene products as required, and would go for weeks sometimes without toilet paper, soap, or feminine hygiene products because there was no staff available to distribute them. Though these situations are not indicative of all state facilities around the country, more often than not, these and other issues do plague the vast majority of state-run institutions.

PRIVATE PRISONS ARE FOR-PROFIT FACILITIES

Conversely, private prisons are for-profit facilities that claim to save the state money and offer inmates more options for learning, safer living environments, rehabilitation, higher quality food, and air conditioning in the dorms. Though both private prisons and state prisons struggle with understaffing, there are some notable differences between the two when it comes to food, safety, and dorm conditions. Incarceration at private prisons is generally better between the two when it comes to food, safety, and dorm conditions. Food at private prisons is generally better, and more is given. Though during the time I have been incarcerated, the portions have decreased significantly, the food is still better than the state offerings.

Another big money maker for prisons was the introduction of computer tablets for the inmate population. Though not all states and prisons have provided tablets to their inmates, those who have participated have gained another revenue stream because of all the fees from services offered. Because of the access to things like email, music, e-books, and games, tablets have been a huge benefit for inmates. Having a tablet to send emails has enabled me to write two books. It also allows me to keep in touch with my family and children. Tablets are so popular in prison that inmates will pay hundreds of dollars to replace theirs should they break or get stolen.

Another reason tablets have been so popular is that inmates have discovered how to break the tablet's security and access social media and internet sites using their tablets. Though the companies providing the services tried to update the security for the tablets, hackers in the free world would send the information to those on the inside in order to circumvent the new security measures and ensure their access to the internet could continue. The facilities, after realizing inmates were accessing the facility Wi-Fi, took measures to keep inmates off the internet. However, inmates then shifted to using hot spots provided by their smartphones to continue to get access to the internet and social media. Because the companies supplying the tablets could not prevent inmates from getting onto the internet and other restricted services, the state has stopped issuing tablets and is no longer providing them to facilities. Private prisons continue to benefit from the outside vendors charging higher prices to inmates and their families who use the tablets, often many times higher than they charge to those outside prison walls.

Safety is also significantly better in private prisons. They do not typically house as many high-security inmates, and this reduces the risk of violent incidents among the inmate population. Though prisons everywhere have problems with violence, state facilities house the worst offenders. Those who have served time in state camps call private prisons a daycare compared to what state prisons are like in relation to violence and the dangers posed to other inmates. Personal safety is a big reason why inmates want to get away from state facilities and go to private camps. I witnessed this when I was at the diagnostic camp that is run by the state. Violence and poor living conditions were evident the moment I arrived.

Living conditions are also greatly improved in private camps versus state camps. Private prisons offer air conditioning, which is a huge benefit during the summer months. Many of the private facilities offer newer buildings, better clothing, better mats to sleep on, and cleaner living environments. State-run facilities have a reputation for being overrun with rodents and insects, filthy living environments, and older buildings where the utilities break down on a regular basis. Private camps offer better and newer facilities; however, if something breaks down, prison management is hesitant to fix or spend money to replace damaged items. One example of this was our air conditioning. The area where I am currently serving my sentence is extremely hot during the summer and fall months. Temperatures can exceed 100 degrees with very high humidity much of the summer. The air conditioner for our unit started to break down and eventually stopped working altogether. This left our dorm with no air circulating, and humid and damp conditions prevailed. This lasted for nearly two and a half years before a new unit was put in to fix the problem. During those two years, we had to endure two summers with temperatures in the dorm exceeding 95 degrees on many occasions.

Complaints to the facility came from inmates and their families, but they were told the dorm temperatures were in the 70s and that the air was working—which was completely untrue. They lied to us and to our families repeatedly telling us a new unit was ordered and coming soon. They did this for over two years until it was finally replaced. Though private prisons are better overall, their hesitancy to spend money on needed repairs led to many years of suffering in our dorm.

EDUCATIONAL OPPORTUNITIES

Private prisons also claim they offer more educational opportunities for inmates to get a GED, learn a trade or craft, and take self-help classes designed to help change delinquent behaviors. Although it is true that they offer these classes on paper, the reality is these classes are just another way for the prison to make money. State and federal funding for the classes is based on attendance. Most of the classes are taught by inmates while the instructor sits and observes in the back. Very little effort is made to teach and to instruct, and most require inmates to show up to class only to sign in so the prison gets credit for having the class that day. Most of the classes I have taken while in prison have been this way. Others I have spoken with have had similar results. The fact is most faculty do not teach or take these classes seriously and are here simply to get easy pay for very little work. Because inmates can tell that there is little time or energy invested in these classes, most get very little from the classes offered and do not sign up for any of the educational opportunities that are offered without an incentive to do so.

SUMMARY

Though neither the state nor private camps offer inmates an ideal situation, private camps are generally safer, have better food, and are less volatile than state facilities. Those who go to private camps will pay more to get clothing, food, and services provided. However, overall safety and standard of living make it a better choice for most. Another big factor to consider when evaluating the merits between a state camp and a private camp is the medical care. The following chapter will give insights into the standard of healthcare in prison and relate stories from those who have had to rely on prison healthcare while incarcerated. But I can assure you, the last thing you want to have in prison is a healthcare problem.

Chapter 12

Prison Healthcare

PRISON MEDICAL CARE

B oth private and state facilities struggle to provide adequate healthcare to inmates. Due to the high cost of medical treatments, prison medical care provides only what is necessary or required by law. That means that if someone is diagnosed with a disease, that person will be treated only once the disease has progressed to where the inmate can no longer function independently. To further cut costs, prisons often hire doctors and nurses who cannot be employed in other healthcare facilities because of malpractice suits and substandard work performance. However, many costs are preventable if the prisons would provide more opportunities to exercise, offer higher quality food, stock healthier commissary options, and maintain a cleaner living environment. For those going to prison, the following is what you can expect in the three areas that most impact your health and wellness. I will explain how the prison system currently handles these problems and what you can do to avoid having issues in these areas.

LIVING CONDITIONS

Dorms in prison are often filthy, allowing sickness and disease to run rampant. The reasons behind this vary. Some in the dorms do not shower, wash their clothing, or keep their lockers or living areas clean, falling victim to insects and other organisms that flourish in filth. Staph infections are also common in dorms and are easily spread by touching a surface infected people have touched. Another issue is that prisons try to save money by diluting the chemicals given to dorms to clean and disinfect the common areas, thereby allowing germs and bacteria to remain and wreak havoc. Shower areas and sinks are overrun with black mold, soap scum, trash, and drug paraphernalia that only compounds the problem. The prison officials do not do enough to ensure inmates do at least the minimum to maintain their health and instead rely on other inmates to get others in line. This usually means that those who do not take care of themselves are eventually threatened with physical harm if they do not clean themselves up. But for some, not even the threat of violence will get them to change their ways. All of these factors greatly impact healthcare and add more costs to the prison's bottom line.

FOOD QUALITY

Another area where prisons cut corners is the quality of food. Those who work in the kitchen report that the meat, in particular, is concerning. The packaging of the meat products states that they are not for human consumption and have a terrible smell when cooked and prepared. Prisons regularly purchase and serve food that cannot be sold to the general public because it does not meet the standard for nutritional quality. Animal byproducts are often what is served instead of actual meat. Prisons are also notorious for serving brown and wilted salad with no salad dressing, old moldy bread, vegetables that have been cooked and reheated so many times that they no longer maintain their shape and instead turn to mush, and watered-down food and condiments that no longer have taste. Another common problem is that the prison does not provide the required food based on the posted menu. Often, items on the menu are not provided, or a cheaper alternative is given, so the offerings are even less substantial. This combination of poor-quality food, smaller portions, and substandard meat and protein options heavily contributes to the unhealthy prison population.

Commissary is another contributing factor to the poor health of inmates. A large portion of the prison population takes medication to manage preventable diseases like heart disease, diabetes, and high blood pressure. Because the commissary is full of items that are filled with sugar, saturated fats, salt, and items with very little nutritional value, it is no surprise that many inmates begin to experience health problems after coming to prison. The lack of healthy options and the high expense of the few somewhat healthy items also contribute to the problem. Until prisons provide more nutritional food and healthier commissary options, inmate health will continue to suffer and will keep the healthcare costs for the prisons high. Prisons would be wise to invest in healthier food and commissary options because it would drastically reduce healthcare costs for inmates having fewer medical issues because of a poor diet. At the same time, those who come to prison need to be aware of these factors and be prepared to watch what they eat, get plenty of exercise, and try to purchase healthier items from the commissary.

EXERCISE OPPORTUNITIES

Exercise is also lacking for most inmates currently serving prison terms. Because adequate staffing at facilities is a problem, inmates are not allowed outdoors to exercise regularly. This leads to a significant problem of obesity. In the facility I am housed in, I can count on two hands the amount of times we have been allowed to exercise in four years! We are told it is due to staffing shortages, but management has had four years to figure it out and is still not consistent about letting us out. This leaves inmates with few options to get adequate exercise in their dorms. Because of the cramped conditions, most inmates are discouraged from exercising indoors. But the longer you go without exercise, the harder it is to get back to it. Many say they exercise regularly on the street but then do nothing during their prison time to stay healthy or to maintain good health. Those who fall into this trap are lazy, sedentary, and sick. Eventually, this leads to being treated for various medical conditions brought on by the lack of physical exertion and exercise. The bottom line is that if you don't exercise while in prison, your health will deteriorate quickly, and you will have health problems sooner rather than later.

PRISON HEALTHCARE EXAMPLES

To illustrate the problem, the following stories are from people whom I have met during my time in prison. Their struggles with their health and the medical care they received illustrate why it is vital to do all you can to avoid health problems while serving your time.

Inmate With Tumor

The first story is of a man who had a tumor in his groin area the size of a softball that made it difficult for him to walk or move without pain. He had put in numerous requests to be seen by the doctor. Still, prison healthcare requires you to go through numerous nurse or nurse practitioner visits and various band-aid treatments before seeing a licensed doctor or physician. This process took over a year before a doctor could see him. In the meantime, the nurses told him that they could not help him but that he could help himself by losing weight. They also made jokes at the inmate's expense and insulted him because of where the large tumor was located. After numerous grievances and complaints to the warden in charge of healthcare, he finally received approval to go to an off-site doctor to get evaluated. The doctor recommended he be scheduled for surgery immediately, saying he was at risk of impotence and causing irreparable harm if the tumor was not removed. Nevertheless, in spite of the doctor's recommendation, prison officials made him wait several more months before the surgery was actually done. Afterward, he was brought back to the prison, where healthcare workers were to follow up with post-operative care; however, the nurses did not check up on him, resulting in complications. Eventually, the area healed, but not until years later. All of this could have been avoided if the prison had been more responsive to his needs early on and given adequate care upon returning from surgery. However, prisons that are only in business to make money do not want to give or offer treatment that is medically necessary because they do not want to spend the money to take care of inmates. Instead, they offer creams, ointments, or pain medicine that only masks the symptoms while not caring for the underlying problem.

Inmate With A Body Rash

My next story illustrates just how far prisons will go not to treat or cure patients in their care. A man I have lived next to for the past four years has had a persistent body rash since coming to prison. His entire body is covered in red splotches, and he constantly needs to scratch himself all day long. Doing this leads to open wounds and bleeding. Time after time, he has gone to get treatment; each time, he comes back with a different ointment, which turns out to be a steroid cream that simply takes away the redness but does not treat the cause of the rash. According to the labels on these various steroid creams, they are only supposed to be used for a few weeks at a time, and then the person using them needs to take a break to allow the body a chance to rid itself of the chemicals that get absorbed into the skin. Prolonged usage can be harmful to the person if used more than recommended. However, this man has been given these creams and told to use them daily by medical professionals for the past four years! His rash has not gone away, and the redness only temporarily goes away while the medication is on the skin. After a few hours, it comes right back—often worse than before. He has spent hundreds of dollars and countless trips to the prison doctors, nurses, and physician assistants who all refuse to treat this man properly. I am not a medical expert, but this rash seems to be some fungus and could be treated if properly diagnosed and given the proper medication. However, giving him the correct medication is more expensive;

therefore, prisons instead recommend treating the symptoms rather than the root cause. By doing so, they put this man at risk of other medical issues by overusing these creams. This is just another example of many where inmates are being given medication to mask the real problem instead of treating the cause. By doing so, they put this man at risk of other medical issues by overusing these creams.

Inmate With A Stomach Tumor

This neglect has been happening to another man with a large tumor in his stomach for the past three years. He has been to the doctor many times and never had the tumor biopsied to find out if it was cancerous or what kind of growth he had. Instead, the prison gave him pain medication to mask the symptoms and allowed him to suffer. There has been no attempt made to diagnose his problem, just medications given to reduce his discomfort.

Sickly Inmate Losing Weight

Another inmate who was in our dorm for a time, who seemed perfectly healthy, suddenly became very sick and started losing weight rapidly. The doctors gave him medications for the symptoms he complained of, but just assumed he had the flu or something similar and dismissed him with pain meds. Over time, he continued to get worse until he was finally taken to a hospital because he could no longer stand up on his own. It was then that tests were done, and hospital staff determined he had cancer—terminal cancer. Because prison staff waited until he was too sick to treat, he died a short time later because they did not treat him sooner.

Poor Dental Care

This "standard care" described thus far also applies to oral dental care. If you have dental problems, you are on a waiting list for months or years before you are seen. Often, the tooth is pulled out. I had a cavity a short time after arriving at my camp and waited three years before they filled it. While fixing it, the dentist said I was fortunate to get it fixed when I did because had I waited any longer, she could not have fixed the tooth. Others in my dorm have had most of their teeth pulled out and are awaiting dentures. The problem with that is it takes several years to get the dentures. In the meantime, you have no way to chew your food. Because teeth cleanings and repairs take so long, most inmates lose their teeth and opt for dentures. If you have a lengthy prison sentence, you better take care of your teeth, or they will be gone by the time you leave.

REMEMBER WARNING

These stories and experiences indicate the standard of care given to those in prison. Often, they will not diagnose problems until it is too late for any medical intervention. If they do diagnose a problem, it is usually too late to treat the problem. If you get cancer or a severe health problem while serving time, you are in serious trouble and might not survive it. Because their standard of care is much lower than you receive in the free world, it is vital to take care of your body in every way you can because it can be a matter of life or death if you do not.

Now that you better understand some of the different aspects of prison, we will discuss in the next chapter what happens daily and how to navigate prison life so you can return home safely to those you love.

Chapter 13

Prison Life

N ow that you know a little about healthcare, commissary, and the differences between state and private prisons, it is now time to learn what daily life is like behind bars. First off, prison is really hard. There is no way to sugarcoat it; every day is complex and has many challenges to overcome.

PRISON SCHEDULE

The first challenge is getting used to the schedule you will follow Monday to Friday each week. In the mornings, you will be awakened early to eat breakfast. When I say early, I mean really early. Most days, breakfast comes between 4 and 5 am. Some days, it comes even earlier. Then, at 6:30 am, you will be awakened and counted standing in front of your bunk. Being counted means, you must stand in front of your bunk while the officers walk through to count the individuals in your dorm or cell house. Once that is done, you can rest until 8 am, when those who have education are allowed to leave for class. Then at 9 am you have inspections. Inspections consist of the warden and his staff coming around to each dorm and walking through inspecting bunks, haircuts, lockers, and general cleanliness. These inspections are supposed to be done Monday to Friday; however, since the pandemic, inspections are the exception, not the rule. More often than not, when we are told to stand for inspections, they never take place.

After inspections are over, you will then be put on standby for lunch. This is usually between 9:30 and 11:00 am. Each prison varies in its schedules, but most are run on the same general timeframe. Going to eat lunch and dinner would seem like pretty harmless events, but often, these walks to the chow hall are dangerous. It is important to always be aware of people gathering in large groups, usually that is when fights and people getting attacked happens. If you see or feel like something might be starting to happen, go back to your dorm and avoid getting caught up in the melee. You don't want to be pepper sprayed or put into segregation because of being an innocent bystander. Being aware and avoiding dangerous circumstances will help you get back home faster.

After lunch, you will be put on standby for another count at noon. You must be in full uniform, something the guards refer to as "state dressed," and standing in front of your bunk or sometimes along the walls. Once the count is over, you have a few hours to yourself. Some like to take a nap, while others exercise, and some work on their cases and appeals. Around 2:30 pm, you will be put on standby again for dinner, usually between 2:30 and 4:00 pm. Then, at 5 pm, you will have another standing count. This is also the time televisions in the dorm are turned on, and you can start to settle in for the evening. In most prisons, multiple televisions are provided so that you have a few options to watch. One television will be for news and movies. The other is dedicated to sports. At night, most will watch the local news or sporting news and movies or shows on the television. Prisons generally offer basic cable packages with sporting channels like ESPN, NFL Network, and others.

After the 5 pm count, there are two more counts before lockdown at 11:30 pm. The first one is at 7:30 pm, and the last standing count is at 10:00 pm. The last count is referred to as a bunk roster count, where you stand in front of your bunk, and the guards come through and check your identification and match it to the paperwork they have. At least, that is what they are supposed to do. Often, they come in and simply check off the paperwork without paying attention to who is standing at the bunk. Because many inmates do not stay in their assigned beds, the staff usually just pretends to look at these sheets as they walk by. As long as the number of inmates matches what they are supposed to have, it is a "good count." The 11:30 pm count is the lockdown count. All inmates must be out of the "day area" in the front of the dorm where the tables and televisions are located. Though not strictly enforced, that is the rule. Weekends work a little differently. Lights come on only for count time, then are turned down to only a dim light, and televisions and phones are on by 8 am.

There are also only two meals on the weekends, and the prison where I am located does not allow us to go to the chow hall on the weekends, presumably because fewer officers are working. No inspections are done on weekends; you do not need to make your bed or be state-dressed. Weekends are your time to relax and have time for yourself. Without the inspections, distractions, and trips to the chow hall, weekends are the time I can get the most done. The prison system here also shows newly released movies on weekends on movie television, so sometimes you have a good movie to enjoy while you relax. During the various sports seasons, many watch games and get loud and obnoxious for their teams. You will also have fights, confrontations over teams, and money wagered on games. You also have those who will want to watch different things things. I learned early on not to get involved with the television; it usually leads to physical confrontations and problems, and no program is worth it.

So now you have a general idea of your schedule during the week and weekends. Now, I want to introduce you to certain elements you will become familiar with in prison. The first one is the gangs that are prevalent in every facility.

GANGS

Not being familiar with gang activities prior to my incarceration, I was surprised when I was locked up to learn how they operate. Gangs greatly influence what goes on in prison in numerous ways. They control the majority of the contraband that comes into facilities, are responsible for much of the violence that takes place, and have an influence on how the facilities are run.

Many gang members were drug dealers before coming to prison and continue to sell while incarcerated. Due to strength in numbers, gangs can control anything from cell phones to tobacco, drugs, and other contraband that comes into the facility. Many times, the people hired to work in prison are affiliated themselves and help these gang members orchestrate hits and deliver drugs to sell. They also allow the gangs to live where they want to live on the compound and turn a blind eye to their violence and bullying. They also police the dorms and exert control over those who would do anything to bring "heat" on them or their business dealings. However, that is not the only way gangs make their money in prison.

Many gangs also use extortion schemes to finance their operations. One of those schemes involves kidnapping other inmates, taking them to their cells, beating them, and then calling their families and showing them pictures of their loved ones beaten. They warn families that further harm will come to them unless they are paid. Once, they even threatened to pull one tooth every hour from an inmate until they received payment. Then, once they get their money, they call back and ask for more later on. If families refuse to pay, their loved ones get gravely hurt and even sometimes killed.

Another scheme they use targets people using burner cell phones. They obtain call lists of specific areas and research the names of the judges and police chiefs in those areas. Then, numerous people call, claiming to be one of those representatives of the court. They claim the person owes a fine due to a missed court date and will be held in contempt unless the fee is paid right then. They keep the person on the phone until payment is received using one of many cash applications available at stores or online. Once the payment is confirmed, they call the next person. I overheard one inmate brag about making $25,000 to $50,000 daily using this scam. Generally, scams target older people who are less aware of these scams and are easily manipulated. However, these scams are so convincing many fall victim to them.

Gangs also extort people in the dorms they live in. They purposely target the weak or those with disabilities and have some of their members threaten them with harm unless they are paid from their commissary each week. They tell these victims not to go to the police or tell others in the dorm, or they will find them and hurt them. Because gangs have members all over the compound and in other prisons, those who are threatened end up paying to avoid getting injured. Also, because of the number of members in dorms at any given time, fighting is futile. For those who have mental health challenges, small statures, or drug addictions, the gangs often target these types to sell to, to extort, and to take advantage.

Gangs also have a lot of influence on how facilities operate. Wardens often speak to gang leadership when they want to figure out ways to reduce violence, drug problems, or gang wars. They often work out deals that work for the warden and the gangs. This allows the gangs to have a certain amount of contraband that prison management will not interfere with if the gangs help to reduce the violence and unrest in the prisons. These deals are made more often than people realize. One of the gang leaders in my dorm currently speaks often with facility leadership, and they speak to him when they need his help with things. In turn, they turn a blind eye to their drug trade and other contraband that they want to hang onto. Though those in charge of these facilities would not openly acknowledge these deals, I know from experience that they happen and that the system is corrupt.

Because of the numbers and influence gangs can exert, it is best to be on good terms with those members you live with and not give them reasons to have a problem with you. You cannot get away from gangs while in prison, but if you avoid getting into debt, buying drugs from them, or interfering with their business dealings, you stand the best chance of getting by without having problems and may even make a few friends along the way. My workout group includes one gang member who is high up in the hierarchy of his gang. We talk often as we exercise and after spending four years in the same dorm, we have a mutual respect and understanding of one another. He knows who I am and what I believe, and he respects that. While in prison, respect goes a long way. So be respectful, stay in your own lane, and focus on what you need to do to get home, and you will make it in one piece.

DRUGS

The next element you will be dealing with is inmates with addictions. Drugs are very prevalent in prison. Those coming in with addictions often have a difficult time functioning day to day. Methamphetamine and synthetic marijuana, called "strips," tobacco, and alcohol permeate almost every dorm to some extent. Some of these drugs are laced with other drugs that can be deadly. For those who have addictions to these substances, prison life is hard and dangerous. Most addicts will sell everything they have just to get high. Because of this, many only have clothing on their backs, no soap or toilet tissue, and no way to clean themselves. Their bed areas are filthy; they don't shower, brush their teeth, or wash their bedding, and they generally stink. When they are not trying to get high, they sleep. For all these reasons, they are often hated in the dorms and are targets for violence, abuse, and extortion. One man in my dorm right now gets high each day, and every time he does, he gets beaten up, abused, mocked, and is a target for anyone wanting to let out their frustrations.

People get frustrated with those with addictions because they have terrible hygiene, do not clean up after themselves, and often try to steal from other inmates to be able to get drugs. Everyone in the dorm is affected by the drug and alcohol abuse that goes on. Just a word of warning to those who struggle with drug use: prison is not the place to come to use drugs. Those who do are easy targets to get extorted, abused in all ways, and hurt. Stay away from this element if your goal is to come home as quickly as possible. This element of prison life only extends your time due to the very real possibility of more charges for drug possession, theft, or violence toward other inmates. If your goal is to go home as quickly as possible and safely, stay away from the drugs while you do your time.

THE GOOD ELEMENT

There are typically three types of people in prison: the ones who are guilty and admit it, those who did it but blame everyone else, and, lastly, those who are innocent and do not fit in with the true criminal element. This last group is the one I feel most comfortable with because it is where I fall in this spectrum. Since I came to prison, I have met many men who, like me, claim they are innocent of the crimes they have been convicted of. Many have shared their stories of injustice with me, and I feel it is appropriate to share some of them in my book. These stories need to be told to show the patterns that exist in the criminal justice system and how they fail to protect the innocent.

Inmate #1 Story

The first story is of a man incarcerated one year before I was. He was convicted of the same crime and had many interesting details in his case. He had been friends with the alleged victim for several years. He had dated another girl who lived at the same address also. When the incident took place, he says it was consensual and not unlike any other time he had been with her. However, for some reason, the next day, she claimed it was rape. Immediately after reporting this, and with no evidence to substantiate her story other than her words, the detective on the case contacted his employer and told his boss her side of the story, resulting in his termination. The police then obtained a warrant for his DNA, which he submitted upon request. After collecting it, the detective dropped the DNA swab on the floor and contaminated the swab. More sloppy investigative work was done, and this man ended up on trial for rape.

It came out afterward that the district attorney for the state had been the family attorney for the alleged victim in the past, thereby creating a conflict of interest. However, he did not remove himself as he should have and tried the case, resulting in a conviction. But once the jury read the verdict, the judge turned and said to the convicted man, "Young man, you need to file an appeal immediately." The judge had tears in his eyes because he knew the man was innocent. A year later, the same judge overturned the case; at that time, he said the evidence did not support a conviction. Here are some reasons the judge felt there was a lack of evidence: 1) The sloppy detective work and lack of professionalism in the case. 2) The accuser's story did not match the facts of the case and continually changed during the investigation. 3)The DNA found at the scene was smaller than a pin drop and from sheets he had slept on with the accuser numerous times. 4) Prosecutorial misconduct was evident because the prosecutor had a relationship with the accuser's family.

There are other details I could have also listed, but I think you get the idea. Investigations nowadays are not done well, are sloppy, and as soon as the prosecution gets a person in their sights, they lock onto them and make the evidence fit the crime rather than letting it lead to the truth. Prosecutors just want convictions, not the truth, and not what is right. This was evident in his case when they brought charges a second time in front of another judge, and they convicted this man again. Now, he is preparing a habeas corpus to try to overturn his case again. There are some significant issues in his case, but rather than let him go, they prosecuted him again. Now, he has been in prison for ten years.

Inmate #2 Story

Another man with the same conviction had an even more troubling case. He was a driver for a ride-share company and had been called to pick up a woman who had been kicked out of a bar for aggressive behavior. She and her friends had been barhopping all day, and because of her behavior toward the bouncers, she finally had to be escorted out of the bar. Her friends said they were fed up with her but waited with her until the ride-share driver arrived to pick her up. Then, these other women went back into the bar.

Upon arriving at her apartment complex, she became aggressive and began to initiate a sexual encounter. He did not know this woman and was initially surprised at how quickly she initiated things with him. She was the aggressor and began touching him and eventually had sex with him. One month later, detectives contacted him and asked him about a woman who claimed her ride-share driver raped her. Confused about why they contacted him, he told them he was unaware anyone had been attacked. They asked him to come in to answer a few questions, and he answered them. Once he arrived, they immediately tried to get him to admit he thought she was attractive and that he had attacked her. Only toward the end of the interview did they read him his rights and then arrested him. They never did advise him of his right to have an attorney present during questioning. Later on, the interrogation tape showed the detective admitted that no matter what this man said when he came in, they would arrest him.

After his arrest, a DNA sample was taken, and the results were not disclosed until the day of his trial two years later. The results of the DNA swab were telling—it was not his DNA. After his arrest, he was given a bond and was free for two years while awaiting trial. However, the prosecution tried its best to get him locked up by requiring him to submit to drug tests and monthly role calls in court. They refused to believe he did not drink and hoped he would somehow miss a role call and find any excuse to lock him up. However, instead, he showed up to take the tests and each role call and remained free until trial.

At the trial, many details came to light that should have led to an acquittal. However, as happens so often now at trials, the prosecution's ability to call frivolous witnesses who are only there to smear the defendant and demonize him ended up trumping the truth and resulted in this man's conviction. Here are some of the more troubling facts from the case that should have given the jury some pause but did not: 1) The DNA taken from the accuser was not from the defendant. Someone else had sex with this woman that night, and they never investigated who this other person was or his connection to the case.

How can you convict a man of rape when it was not his DNA found in the woman? 2) The defendant used a condom, and the woman who accused him of assaulting her helped him put it on before their encounter. How does someone who claims she was raped willingly help to put the condom on her attacker? 3) The defendant who drove the rideshare was not with the accuser when she was out drinking and had no way of knowing how much she drank or her level of intoxication. He said she appeared normal when he picked her up, could give him accurate directions, and did not stumble or display any impairment. 4) One of his jurors sent an email to the judge claiming he was a friend of the prosecutor from church. The prosecutor was not removed from the case even though a clear conflict of interest was present with this juror. 5) The friends of the victim claimed she drinks excessively all the time, and it was normal behavior for her. 6)) Medical reports showed no indication of an attack taking place and could find no evidence of sexual assault. 7) The accuser claims she did not remember climbing on top of the defendant and could not remember what happened that night. However, when questioned by her attorney, she could remember most of the details of the night except the sexual encounter. However, when cross-examined, she claimed to have very little recollection of the events she had just testified to.

For these and other reasons, this case lacked any evidence a crime was committed. Instead of thoroughly investigating the case and locating the person whose DNA was present in the victim, they charged and convicted an innocent man who was the real victim and gave him 35 years for something he did not do.

Inmate #3 Story

This final story is hard to hear but is also indicative of how far prosecutors will go to protect themselves and to avoid the embarrassment of wrongful prosecution. This man was 60 when he finally found a woman whom he loved and married. This woman had a 12-year-old daughter and when they married, they moved into a farmhouse owned by this man. Shortly after they married, he found out his stepdaughter was using drugs. He confronted her and told her she could not use drugs in his home. Angered by this, she decided to go to the police and falsely accused this man of touching her inappropriately. He was subsequently arrested and later convicted. He was given 65 years in prison. During his appeal, this girl started going to church and changed her life. This transformation also brought about a need to correct the wrong she had done to this innocent man. So she contacted the prosecutor and gave a sworn affidavit that she had lied about the abuse and did so because he would not allow her to use drugs in his home.

She also stated she was willing to accept the consequences for lying, including prosecution. However, the prosecutor decided that her confession was not real and instead believed what she said back when she was 12 and using drugs. He refused to reopen the case and instead let the conviction stand. Even when the victim came forward to admit she lied and her reasons for doing so, the prosecution refused to allow this man to go free. Though this new evidence can be used to help exonerate him eventually, he has lost his marriage, job, home, and reputation and years of his life all because of false witness testimony that ended up being recanted years later. There never was any physical evidence that the girl had been abused. He was convicted solely on this young girl's testimony.

Chapter 14

Prepare for Life After Prison

At last, you are getting to the final stages of your prison stay, and the prospect of going home is right in front of you. Admittedly, this part of my book relies heavily on those who have already gone home and, in some cases, come back. Their stories helped me to understand that going home is a big adjustment; if you want to stay out of prison, then changes have to be made in prison in order to avoid making the same mistakes in the future. These next few sections will outline the steps that you want to take and also avoid keeping yourself from being part of the 85 percent of those who return to prison after serving their sentences.

CHANGE BEHAVIORS

Sounds simple enough, right? Just stop doing what you were doing before and you will not end up back in prison. But in reality, for most, it is not. The reasons for this are understandable and predictable. All who come to prison and spend years behind bars develop bad habits that make going back to the real world a challenge. Prison life is sedentary, without jobs and responsibilities. There is very little required other than to get up for inspections, go to eat, and stand up for counts. Aside from that, inmates determine how they spend their time and how productive they are. Most struggle with managing their time wisely and taking advantage of the opportunities available to them to further their educations or to learn a trade. Instead, many feed their addictions, play cards, sleep, or spend their time watching television or reading books. Though some of those things are not necessarily bad, they also do not help you get back out in the world. Instead, because they wasted their time in prison and did not improve themselves or their situations, many inmates go back to the same environments, people, and circumstances they left initially, making it difficult to change their ways because of old habits. Others do not have trade or work experience and resort to stealing, selling drugs, or other illegal options to support themselves. Consequently, inmates find it difficult to change their ways. In addition, others do not have family or support on the outside and go back to what they know because it is all they feel they can do. But whatever the circumstances are, you need to consider changing everything to change your life.

Real change necessitates changing friends, addresses, associations, and everything that contributed to your incarceration. Those who think they can still be friends and associate with those who break the law and they not do it are also only lying to themselves. The numbers do not lie, nor do human behavior and habits. The truth is that if you hang around people who disregard the law, you eventually will, too. The same can be said for those who use drugs or any other behavior that a person has struggled with. You can not be around something you have struggled with in the past unless you want to do it again. Like an alcoholic going to a bar and thinking he can resist taking a drink, how long before he gives in to his weakness? You might resist for a time, but at some point, if you do not get away from bad influences, they will eventually wear you down and endanger your freedom.

I have talked with countless men who have told me how they ended up back in prison, with the overwhelming majority saying it was because they fell back into the same crowds and habits. All of them left determined to never come back, but after a short time, they started to forget their time in prison, got comfortable, and then back into their old ways. Not long afterward, they were arrested and sent back to the same prisons they left. I have seen several men who left and came back, and it always amazed me at how little time it took for them to re-offend.

The bottom line is that in order to change your life, you have to change what you want, where you live, and with whom you associate. To do this it requires a lot of help, work, and a good support system. The following are some suggestions on ways to break out of old habits, make new friends, and create a whole new life.

CHURCH AND RELIGION

For those who are religious and those who have never learned about God or what they believe, going to church and befriending those you meet can help you stay on the right path and start over. Many churches offer services and assistance to those who are willing to return to school, learn a trade, or find employment. Going to church also helps people turn to God, who has the power to help people change who they are into the person they need to be. I have personally experienced great changes in my life because I chose to ask God for help, and I feel He gave me the strength and the power to make the necessary life changes.

PLANS AND GOALS

Another important part is to have a plan or goals to achieve upon release. It is hard to know where you are going if you do not know how to get there. Having a plan helps you to decide what you need to do and how you will ultimately do it. Then, you can move forward with confidence and find a good job, a safe place to live, and people who can help you get re-established. Making plans and preparing for your release will help ensure you do what is required to maintain your freedom. This provides you with a sense of purpose and accomplishment; each is important to help you have the confidence you need to begin your new life.

BREAK HABITS

The following are some suggestions for breaking old habits, making new friends, and creating a new life.

Transitional Center

Another way many prepare for their new life is by going to a transitional center if the state you live in allows for this option. Where I am currently incarcerated, they offer these centers to allow inmates to start working again and earning an income so that they have money and recent work experience once released. These centers are strict with their rules and enforcement, and any violations will result in going back to prison to finish your sentence. Normally, these centers allow inmates who are 3 to 18 months away from being released to request a transfer to one of these facilities. Depending on the nature of your offense and other factors, there may be only certain facilities available. So, it is important to request a transfer as soon as you qualify in order to have the best chance to go. These places offer inmates more freedom and a taste of what being back in society will look like. Inmates can often save thousands of dollars during their time in these centers to help them begin their new lives. Often, if an inmate performs well on the job, that experience can lead to a permanent position once the inmate is released. Transitional centers require the inmate to pay a weekly or monthly fee for room, food, and amenities. The fee varies based on where the center is and the state you live in. They also allow inmates to have a cell phone and certain freedoms not had in prison. They will do random drug tests and have strict curfews, so being on time and drug-free is a must. For those who are able to go to these centers, it provides the needed work and financial help to those without family or outside help to begin their transition to life after prison.

Trade Education

Most prisons offer inmates a chance to further their education by offering trade classes, GED credits, and in some cases a college degree. Most jobs today require at least a high school education in order to be hired, so taking the opportunity while incarcerated if you do not have a GED is a must! Having a GED can enable you to get a job once released that would not have been possible without it. It can help you get a higher-paying job and open the door to other possibilities. Because these classes are free and offered to any who are interested, it is important to take advantage of these opportunities to get ahead while serving your time.

Addiction Recovery Centers

Similar to transitional centers, those with addictions can seek help from addiction recovery centers while also working and learning how to adjust to life without drugs. These centers are often difficult to get into, so any mistakes will result in losing your place to someone else who is willing to follow the rules. They do not offer second chances in most cases, so if you fail a drug test or miss a curfew, you will be sent back to prison. For those who want to kick their addictions, these centers can be instrumental in helping to break free from these substances and learn how to live drug-free. Many of these facilities only accept people once they have been released from prison and are willing to adhere to their strict guidelines and procedures. But if you really want to get over an addiction, this is a great place to start.

While staying in the facility, they will provide you with employment opportunities, housing, and drug treatment programs. Once you complete the program, they may provide a chance to work for the facility or keep the job you have had. It provides a new start for those willing to work hard, follow the rules, and stay drug-free. These and other resources are available to those who are preparing to go home. Depending on where you live, other options may also be available to you. The key is to ask questions, find out what your options are, and then have a plan for what you will do once you are released. If you do, you will be part of the 15 percent who do not come back because you were prepared, had a plan, and worked to achieve your goals.

Chapter 15

Conclusion

It is sobering to know that the system as it stands today is not what it used to be. Those in positions of power tend to abuse their power to further their self-interest, denying justice to those who are wronged and sending many who are innocent to prison. The criminal justice system only works properly if those in positions of power are people of integrity and character. James Madison once said that democracies only work if the people are moral people. I believe that especially applies to our justice system.

Knowing this to be the case, those who go through the system today should know the fight is as much about what you do to protect your rights and knowing what those rights are as it is about truth and justice. Attorneys, judges, and police all use their positions to intimidate, coerce, and manipulate to accomplish their purposes. As is the tendency of most people, once given some authority, they immediately use it in ways that are not right and unjust. So, if you do not know your rights and how the process works, you will fall victim and be taken advantage of by your ignorance of the laws and statutes.

To prevent being like so many who have gone before, I hope those who read my book will be better prepared to handle situations involving the justice system should they ever find themselves being investigated for a crime. One in ten people in this country will go to prison or know someone who has. Even those who think they will never have to worry about dealing with the justice system at some point may be faced with defending themselves against false accusations. It happened to me, and it can happen to anyone.

My advice is to know what to expect, find out the laws and procedures where you live, and make sure you do not just assume your lawyer, judge, or the system will eventually get it right. You must ensure the process is fair, your rights are protected, and the people working for you do their job. Your life will depend on it, so you must be fully vested in your case. Above all, remember that only you have a truly vested interest in maintaining your freedom. So, do not let those who do not care if you go free or go to prison decide your fate without you. Take control by insisting you are a part of the process the entire way and do all you can to know the law to ensure the process is done fairly and legally. Doing these things might make the difference between years behind bars and your freedom. If I had done what is suggested in this book, I am confident I would not be here today.

Best of luck in your case! If you are innocent, I hope your knowledge of the system, the laws, and the truth sets you free!

Dedication

I want to thank all who have contributed to this book by sharing their stories, experiences, and truths to help bring awareness to important issues.
I also want to acknowledge the incredible efforts of my mother, who helped make my books a reality.
Finally, I want to thank my family and beautiful children for inspiring me to reach higher, be better, and share what I have learned so that others may benefit.
I genuinely hope that the things I share will help those who come after me to get justice for themselves and their families.

Matthew Harrison

Acknowledgments

This book would not have been possible without the help, patience, and support of many people, including my Mother, who served as my editor, facilitator, and proxy.

I want to thank those with whom I am incarcerated for sharing their experiences and for their encouragement.

I also want to express my gratitude to my family and friends, who have believed in me and supported me throughout my journey.

Last but not least, I want to thank my Heavenly Father and his Son and Savior, Jesus Christ, who helped me do things I never thought possible and inspired me to never give up and, instead, do everything in my power to seek justice and freedom.

Matthew Harrison

About the Author

In *Unraveling Wrongful Conviction and Miscarriage of Justice*, Matthew Harrison bares his soul in a compelling narrative that unfolds against the backdrop of a life shaped by the dichotomy of faith and despair. In the close-knit community of The Church of Jesus Christ of Latter-Day Saints, Matthew's early years were marked by achievements as an Eagle Scout and recipient of the Duty to God award. His athletic prowess, particularly in high school basketball, hinted at a promising future.

Yet, beneath the surface, the specter of divorce cast a long shadow over Matthew's formative years, leaving him grappling with feelings of unlove, unworthiness, and an innate reluctance to trust others. The remarriage of his mother introduced a stepfather whose broken promises and subsequent abuse forced Matthew into a defensive posture, vowing to safeguard his heart at all costs.

Undeterred by early setbacks, Matthew embarked on a journey that included a mission to Portugal, marriages, fatherhood, and successful ventures in business. However, his world crumbled when a wrongful accusation led to a conviction and subsequent incarceration, with an unsuccessful appeal prolonging his time behind bars to nine years and counting.

Unraveling Wrongful Conviction and Miscarriage of Justice lays bare Matthew's struggles, his descent into a double life, and the pivotal moment when false accusations threatened to unravel everything. In despair, he turned to God, experiencing a spiritual rebirth that illuminated a path toward healing and transformation. Despite the confines of prison, Matthew's life continued to be infused with blessings—food, clothing, family support, and a newfound sense of safety and well-being.

Throughout four years of writing, Matthew unraveled the layers of his tumultuous life, aiming to expose the truth concealed by the judicial system and media. Chapter by chapter, he reveals the pain, the choices that led him astray, and the unwavering faith that ultimately guided him toward redemption.

Readers have responded with five-star reviews, captivated by Matthew's resilience in the face of adversity and the remarkable redemption that emerged from the crucible of his experiences. *Unraveling Wrongful Conviction and Miscarriage of Justice* is a testament to the strength of the human spirit, the capacity for change, and the profound impact of faith in the face of life-altering challenges.

In *Judicial Misconceptions Shattered*, Matthew looks to the future, he trusts God with his faith and life, finding peace in repentance and a resolute commitment to move forward, no matter the twists and turns that lie ahead.

Matthew has helped others around him write and read letters and research criminal law. In contrast, continuing research on his own case, he has gathered all he has learned about prison life from his own experiences and from others he has come to know over the last nine years. From arrest to innocence or conviction, to surviving prison life, and eventually preparing to leave prison and start anew, Matthew's goal has been to use his skills, talents, and belief in God to help others. The result is this book, *Judicial Misconceptions Shattered*. What is next for him? Perhaps in researching his own case, he will find a new beginning for him that benefits many others.

He misses his family and looks forward to being released to begin a new life with family members, enriched by his increased understanding and commitment to the Lord, to whom Matthew attributes many blessings these past nine years. In the meantime, his love of reading and helping others sustains him in this difficult environment.

Before you go...

☆☆☆☆☆

Rate this book (Post on Amazon)

Follow the Author: Get release updates, recommendations, and freebies coming soon.

website: https/www.mharrisoninspire.com

Embark on an extraordinary journey of redemption and resilience in *Unraveling Wrongful Conviction and Miscarriage of Justice,* the first book by Matthew Harrison. This riveting memoir is not just a story—it's a roadmap to your transformation.